Houghton Mifflin

SURPRISE

DISCOVER

LITERACY ACTIVITY BOOK

Senior Authors
J. David Cooper
John J. Pikulski

Authors
Kathryn H. Au
Margarita Calderón
Jacqueline C. Comas
Marjorie Y. Lipson
J. Sabrina Mims
Susan E. Page
Sheila W. Valencia
MaryEllen Vogt

Consultants
Dolores Malcolm
Tina Saldivar
Shane Templeton

Houghton Mifflin Company • Boston

Atlanta • Dallas • Geneva, Illinois • Palo Alto • Princeton

Illustration Credits

Leo Abbett 89, 90; Elizabeth Allen 4, 143, 160, 162, 163, 167-170, 198; Shirley Beckes 21, 29, 80, 101, 144, 145, 151-154, 157; Alex Bloch/Asciutto Art Reps 56, 63, 65; Paulette Bogan 41, 47, 50; Ruth Brunke 17, 18, 31, 35, 111, 114; Olivia Cole/Asciutto Art Reps 5, 25-28, 39, 42-46, 57, 58, 66, 71-74, 87, 93, 98, 107, 108, 115, 116, 130, 131, 133, 149, 184, 191, 193, 196; Susanne Demarco/ Asciutto Art Reps 30, 40, 76, 135-138, 178, 187-190; Shelly Dieterichs-Morrison 181; Eldon Doty/HK Portfolio iii, 8, 18, 82; Tom Duckworth 115, 130, 197; Kate Flanagan/Cornell & McCarthy 128, 159, 179, 194; Dave Garbot 81, 126, 183; Patrick Girouard iii, 55, 59, 62, 64; Megan Halsey 86, 95, 97; Robin Michal Koontz 13; Ruth Linstromberg 19; Mas Miyamoto/Square Moon Productions 106; Judith Moffatt iv, 155; Deborah Morse/Square Moon Productions 38, 52, 91, 92; Laurie Newton-King 85, 94, 96; Judith Pfeiffer/ Gwen Walters 164, 172, 173, 185, 195; Jan Pyk/Asciutto Art Reps 22, 34; Sally Springer 75, 84, 13, 118, 123, 124, 134, 142; Lynn Sweat/Cornell & McCarthy 15, 16, 54; Stan Tusan/Square Moon Productions 7, 9-12, 60, 117, 119, 125, 156, 161, 166, 174, 175; Jackie Urbanovic 20, 24, 33, 68, 79; Dave Winter 49, 51, 53, 171, 176.

Photo Credits

©Tony Freeman/PhotoEdit 127; ©H. Armstrong Roberts, Inc. 192; ©Michael Newman/PhotoEdit 177; ©PhotoDisc iii, left, iv, top, 35, 69, 105, top right, bottom right, 120; ©Leonard Lee RueIII/Tony Stone Images 110; ©Stuart Westmorland/Tony Stone Images 150; All other photographs by Ralph J. Brunke Photography.

1997 Impression

Printed in the U.S.A.

ISBN-13: 978-0-395-74365-2 ISBN-10: 0-395-74365-6

25 26 27 28 -1429-12 11 10 09

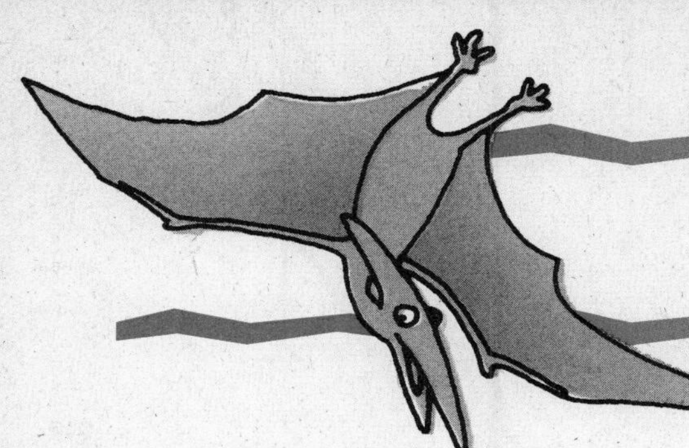

CONTENTS

CONTENTS

MAGIC PICTURES

Consonant Sounds and Letters

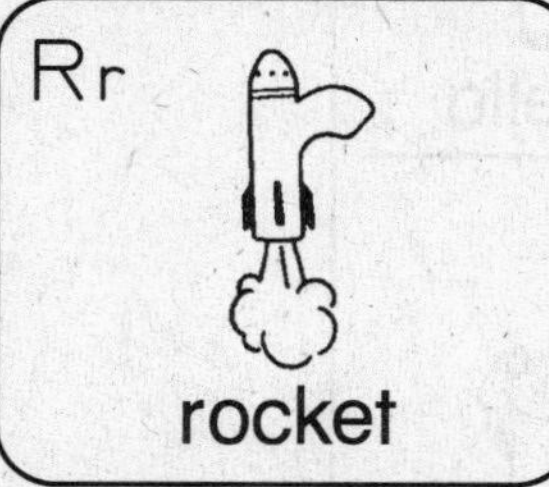

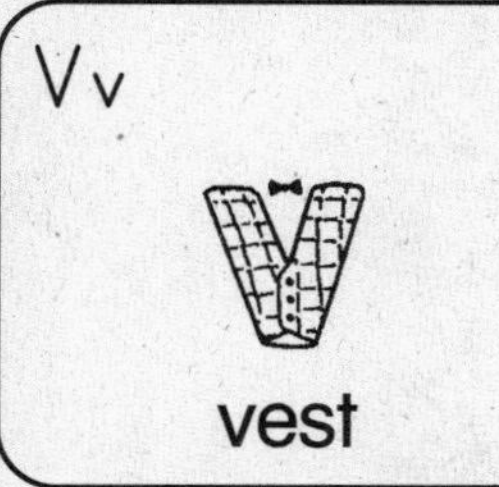

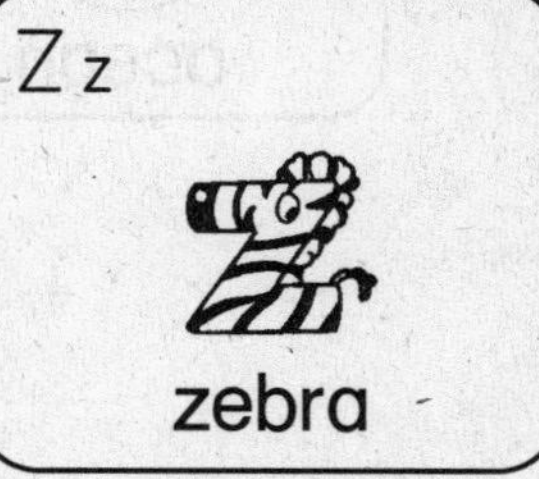

MAGIC PICTURES

Vowel Sounds and Letters

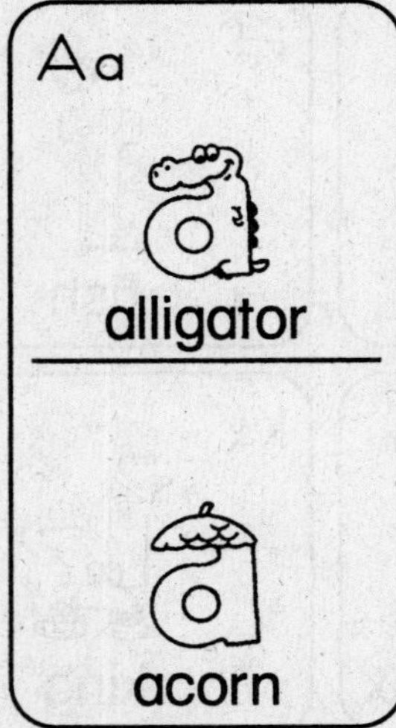

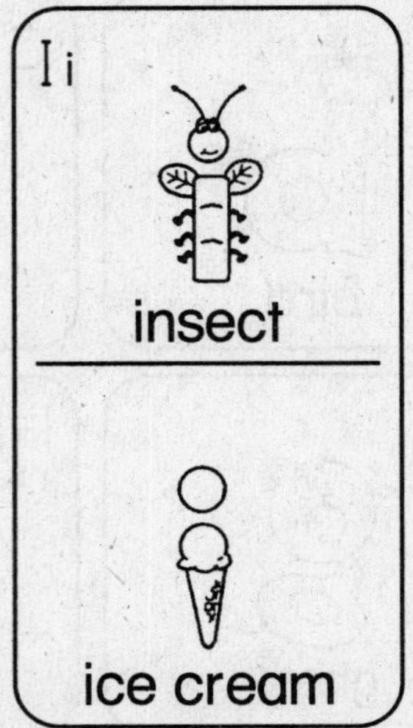

Name

Best Big Brother

Read the story.

My Brother Todd

Todd helps me with my homework. He helps me with the puzzle in the newspaper, too.

We walk to school each day. After school, we go to the playground. At the playground, Todd helps me . . .

Draw and write an ending for the story.

Name ______________________

Do It Together

Draw one thing the older brother does by himself.

What is he doing?

____

Draw one thing the brothers do together.

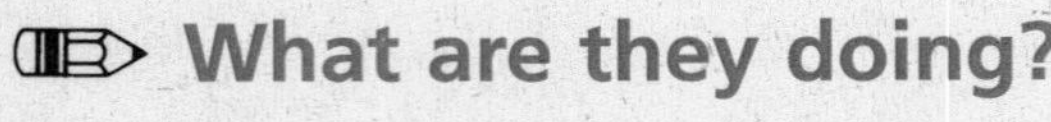

What are they doing?

____

Name

Family, Friends, and Neighbors

Who do you want to write about? Think about people you like to do things with. Write their names.

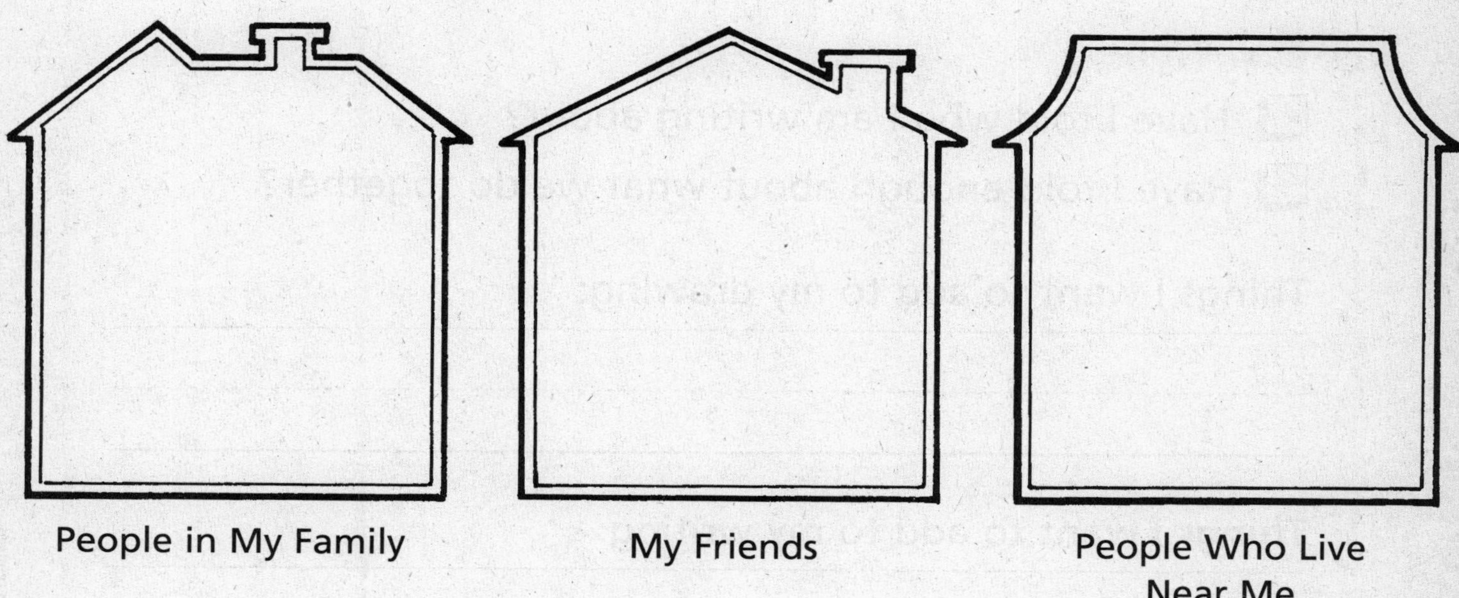

People in My Family

My Friends

People Who Live Near Me

Circle the name of the person you would most like to write about.

What are some things you like to do with that person? Draw or write your ideas.

Name ______________________

Take Another Look

• Revising Checklist •

Ask yourself these questions about what you have done.

- ☐ Have I told who I am writing about?
- ☐ Have I told enough about what we do together?

Things I want to add to my drawing:

____

____

Things I want to add to my writing:

____

____

Questions to Ask My Writing Partner

- What do you like best about my drawing?
- What do you like best about what I have written?
- Is there anything I should add?

Name ____________________

A Chase

Pick two animals from the story.
Then write or draw to complete the chart.

What is the animal?		
What did it look like?		
What did it do?		

Name ______________________

Good Times for Mouse

Tell about the fun Mouse has. Write a word from the box to finish each sentence.

game	gas
slam	skate
plane	plan

1 Mouse likes to go in a ______________.

2 Mouse can ______________.

3 Mouse plays this ______________.

Write your own sentence about Mouse. Use words from the box.

chase	bake
race	snake
ate	cake

"Too late!" said Baby Mouse.
"We ate all the cake!"

"We'll bake again," said Dad Mouse.

(Fold Line)

This Is My Book

Cake for Baby Mouse

"I like cake," said Baby Mouse.
"Will you bake one for me?"

(Fold Line)

Baby Mouse ate the cake.
"Save some for Mom," said Dad Mouse.

Dad Mouse put the cake on a big plate.
Then he put Baby Mouse's name on it.

(Fold Line)

"Yes," said Dad Mouse.
"You and I will make a cake."

Dad Mouse made the cake.

Baby Mouse helped.

(Fold Line)

"Now the cake will bake," said Dad Mouse.

"It will not take too long."

Name

The Great Chase

Fold a piece of paper in half like a book.

Cut and paste one story part on each page in order.

Write or draw your own ending on the last page.

The Great Chase

Jake has a little mouse.
Jake has a cat.
Jake has a big dog too.

1

One day, the little mouse ran away with some cheese.
The cat chased the mouse out the door.
The big dog ran after them.
Jake ran after them all.

2

Lee walked by.
"Stop them, Lee!" called Jake.

3

Name

What Happened?

Think about **EEK! There's a Mouse in the House.**
Write a sentence to answer each question. Use words from the box. Remember to add **ed**.

chase	knock
dance	

1 Who chased the mouse?

2 Who knocked over a lamp?

3 Who danced with a mop?

Name

Surprise!

Write two naming words in each box.

People	Places
Animals	**Things**

Use some of the words to write a sentence about a surprise visit.

Name

The Name of the Game

Each Spelling Word has the long **a** sound. It is the first sound in a.

Spelling Words		
cake	came	late
make	take	name
Your Own Words		

Write each Spelling Word under the correct mouse.

1 ____________

2 ____________

3 ____________

4 ____________

5 ____________

6 ____________

Write the two Spelling Words that begin like ▢.

7 ____________

8 ____________

Name

Spelling Spree

Spelling Words		
cake	came	late
make	take	name

Write the Spelling Word for each clue.

1. It rhymes with **lake**. It begins like 🐱.
2. It rhymes with **frame**. It begins like nurse.
3. It rhymes with **gate**. It begins like 🦁.

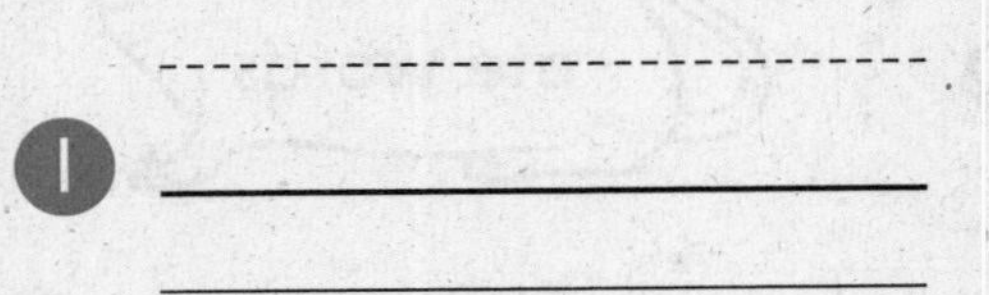

1

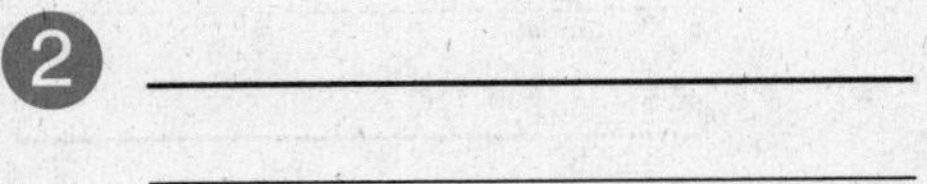

2

3

Circle each Spelling Word that is wrong.
Write it correctly.

4 I kame into the room.

5 I saw a mouse taek the cheese.

6 Should I mayk him stop?

Name ______________________

The Amazing Mouse

Help the mouse find the cheese.

Draw a line to connect the naming words.

room
lamp
to
dog
the
is
girl
send
over
house
that
boy
cow
eat
big
mop
an

Now write each naming word in the chart.

People		
Animals		
Places		
Things		

Name ______________________

The Big Catch

Use words from the box to complete the story.

saw	garage	bait	trouble	sleep

Jane had never fished before. So Dad got a can from

the ______________. He put some good

______________ in it. Then they went fishing.

They had ______________ at the lake. They could not catch even a little fish.

"Do fish ______________?" said Jane. "Or do they just rest?"

Then Jane ______________ a big thing. Could that be a fish?

Name

Put It in Order

Read the sentences about the boy in the story. Then write them in the correct order.

He followed the alligator.

He shut the garage door.

He put food on the floor.

He went to get food.

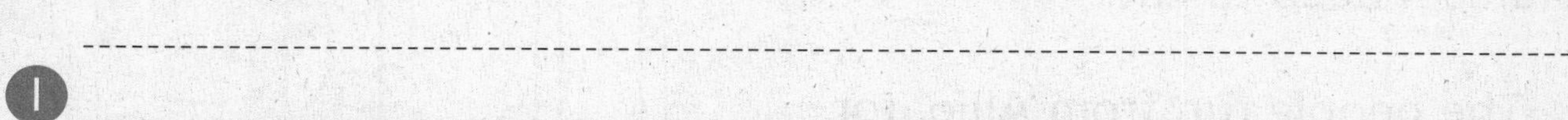

1

2

3

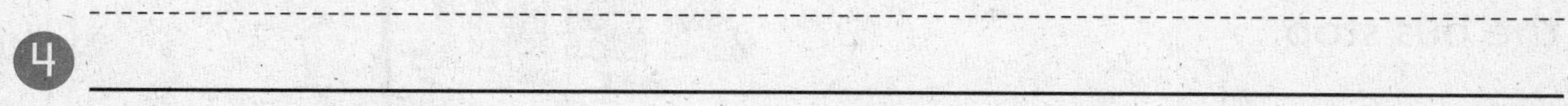

4

On a separate sheet of paper, write or draw some of the foods the boy used as alligator bait.

Name

I'm Hungry

Read this new story about the alligator. Complete the story map on the next page.

Alligator needs something to eat. He walks to the bus stop. There, he sees some people eating.

One man has a plum. Alligator asks, "Can I have your plum? I need to eat."

The people run from Alligator. Alligator will not get that plum!

Then two other alligators get off a bus. They have some buns.

They ask Alligator to sit down with them. The three alligators eat and have a good time at the bus stop.

Name ____________________

Setting (Where?)
Characters (Who?)
Problem (What is wrong?)
Events (How the character tries to solve the problem)
Ending (Is the problem solved? How?) **Tell the story in your own words to a friend.**

Name ______________________

Down the Slide

Read the word at the top of the slide.
Write new words as you go down the slide.
The first one is done for you.

s l i d e

Example: Take out the **l** in **slide**. s i d e

1. Change the **s** to **w**. ① ___ ___ ___ ___

2. Change the **d** to **f**. ② ___ ___ ___ ___

3. Change the **w** to **l**. ③ ___ ___ ___ ___

4. Change the **f** to **k**. ④ ___ ___ ___ ___

That was a great ride!

Now write about another great ride you have had.

"You did it, Kim," said Mom.
"Mike likes the kite.
And he likes your help even more!"

(Fold Line)

This Is My Book

Something for Mike

"Mike is one today," said Mom.
"We need to get him something nice."

"I have five dimes," said Kim.

"I will get something nice for Mike."

(Fold Line)

"But you can help him," said Mr. Pine.

"The price is just five dimes."

"I'll take it!" said Kim.

"This kite is nice," said Mr. Pine.

"The kite is nice," said Kim.
"But Mike is too little to run with a kite."

(Fold Line)

"How can I help you, Kim?" said Mr. Pine.

"I need something for Mike," said Kim.

"This bike is nice," said Mr. Pine.

"The bike is nice," said Kim.

"But Mike is too little to ride a bike."

(Fold Line)

"Mice are nice," said Mr. Pine.

"Mice are nice," said Kim.

"But Mike is too little to have pet mice."

Name ______________________

Go to the Swamp

dog
cake
nut
air
ball

Help Alligator follow the trail to the swamp. Look at each picture. Write a word on the lines to complete each compound word.

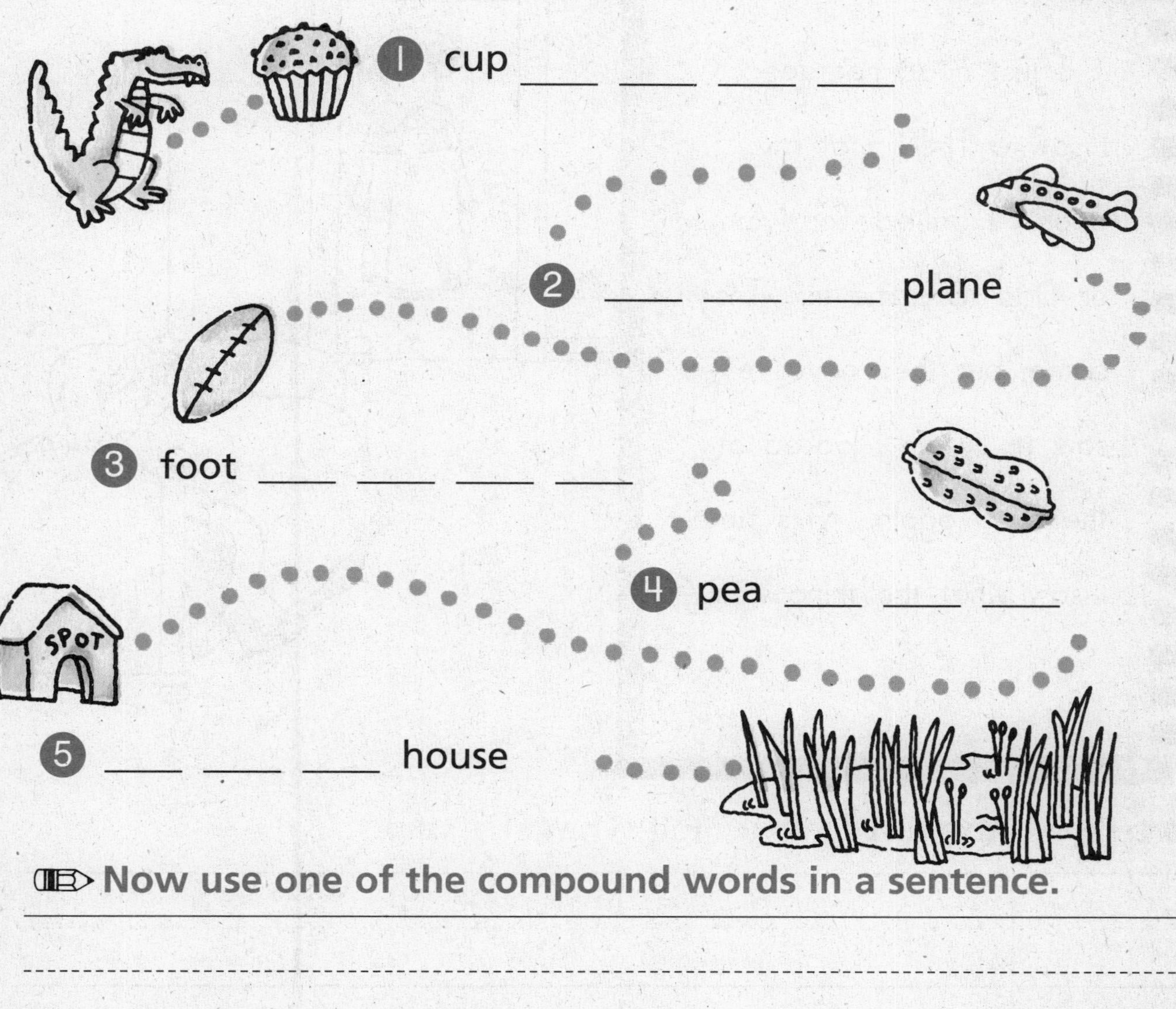

1 cup ___ ___ ___ ___

2 ___ ___ ___ plane

3 foot ___ ___ ___ ___

4 pea ___ ___ ___

5 ___ ___ ___ house

Now use one of the compound words in a sentence.

Name

One Scary Night

This girl thought she saw something scary.
Read what she wrote about it.

I just could not sleep. I saw a THING at my door. I called for Mom or Dad to come in. They came, but they never even saw it. Then I looked at the door again. This time I saw what the thing was!

Finish the girl's story. Tell what she saw.

Name

Where Does It Go?

Look at the house plan. What rooms do you see? What things might you find in each room? Write or draw your ideas in the boxes.

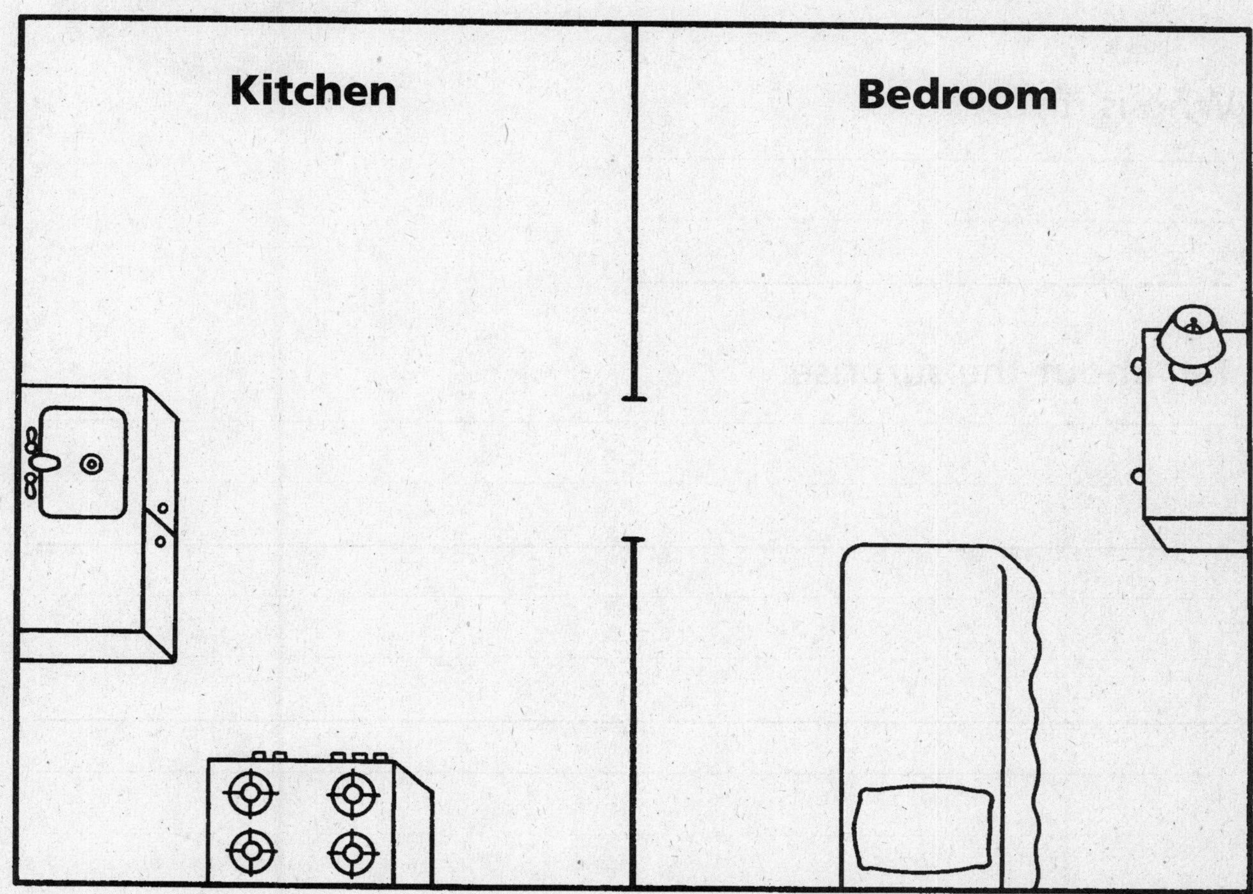

Write a sentence about another room in a house.

Name

Guess Who's Here!

What if you found a surprise guest in your house? Write a message to someone in your family. Tell about the surprise.

Who is it for?

Tell about the surprise.

Sign your name.

Name ______________________________

Pick the Fruits

Spelling Words		
time	hide	five
like	mine	bike

Your Own Words

Each Spelling Word has the long **i** sound. It is the first sound in 🍦.

The alligator can only eat fruit with the 🍦 sound. Color the fruit the alligator can eat.

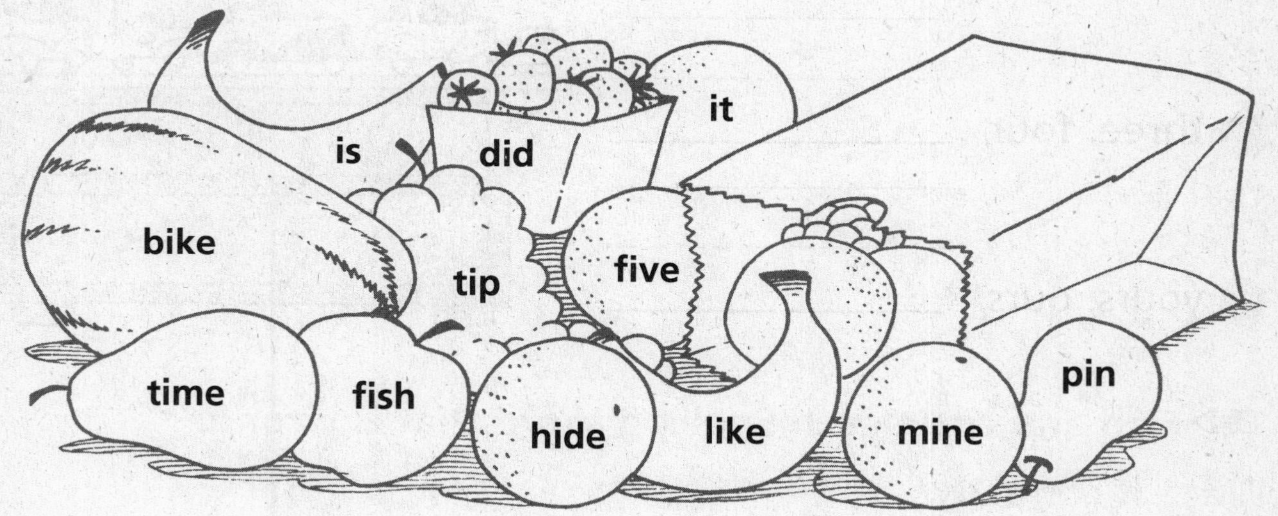

Write the Spelling Words from the fruit you colored.

1 ______________ 3 ______________ 5 ______________

2 ______________ 4 ______________ 6 ______________

Write the two Spelling Words that rhyme with hike.

7 ______________ 8 ______________

Name

Spelling Spree

Spelling Words		
time	hide	five
like	mine	bike

Think how the words in each group are alike. Write the missing Spelling Words.

1. skates, wagon, ______
2. three, four, ______
3. yours, ours, ______

Find and circle each Spelling Word that is wrong. Write it correctly.

4. It is tine for bed. ______
5. I would lik to stay up late. ______
6. Where can I hied? ______

Name ______________________________

Puzzle Fun

Color green the pieces with special names.

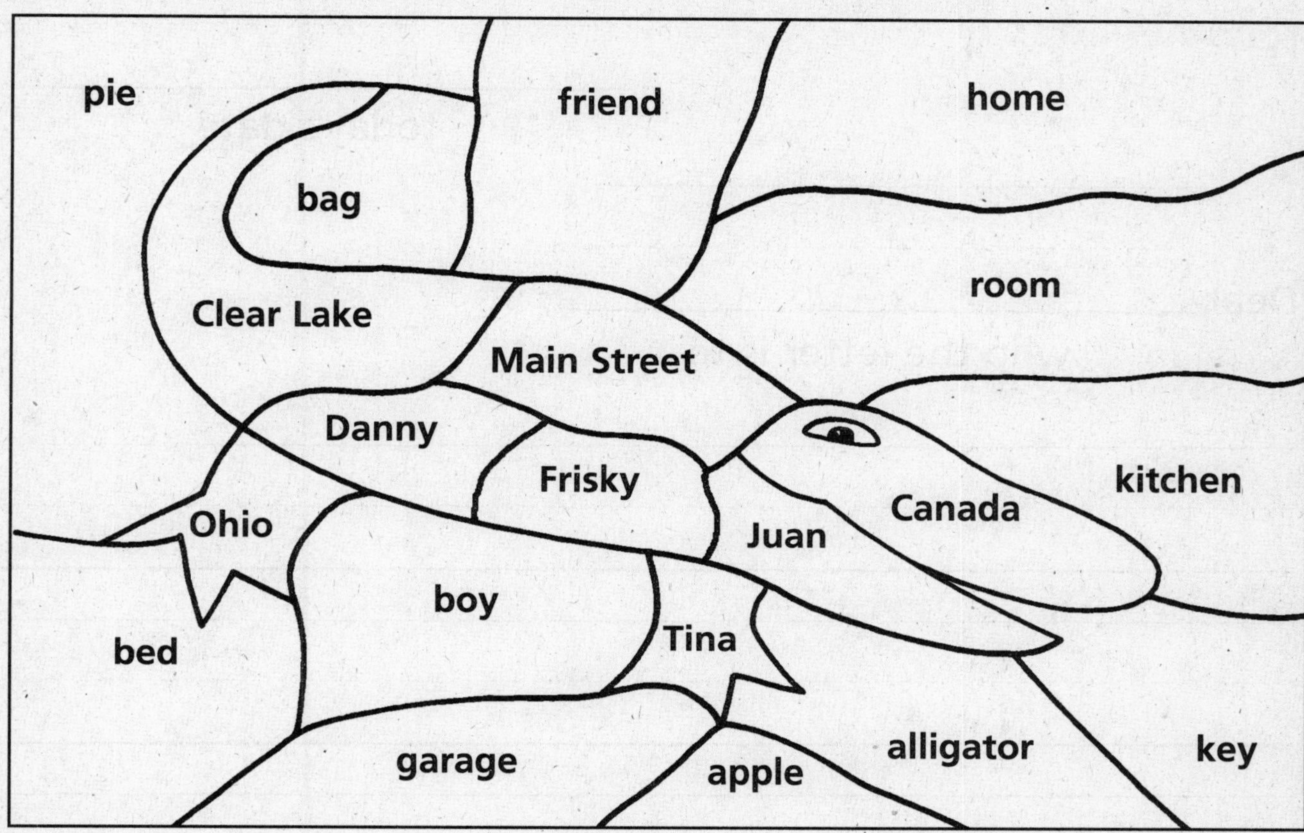

Now write some special names.

1 your name ______________________________

2 a pet ______________________________

3 a street ______________________________

Name

Dear Friend

Write your ideas for your letter.

today's date

Dear ______,

who the letter is to

your closing

your name

Name

Take Another Look

Revising Checklist

Ask yourself these questions.

- ☐ Does my letter make sense?
- ☐ Have I told enough in my letter?
- ☐ Do I want to add anything to make my letter better?

Questions to Ask My Writing Partner

- Is there anything that is not clear?
- Do I need to add anything?
- What do you like best about my letter?

Name

Play Time!

Write words from the box to complete the sentences.

give
ask
old
show
mother
moose

1 We can put on a ______________.

2 I'll be a ______________ eating blackberries.

3 Here are some ______________ antlers.

4 Your ______________ will probably make the scenery.

5 I'll ______________ her to ______________ us a snack too.

Now write what Mother might say.

Name

What the Moose Thought

Look at the pictures. Next to each picture, draw what it made the moose think of.

When the moose saw this, he thought of this.

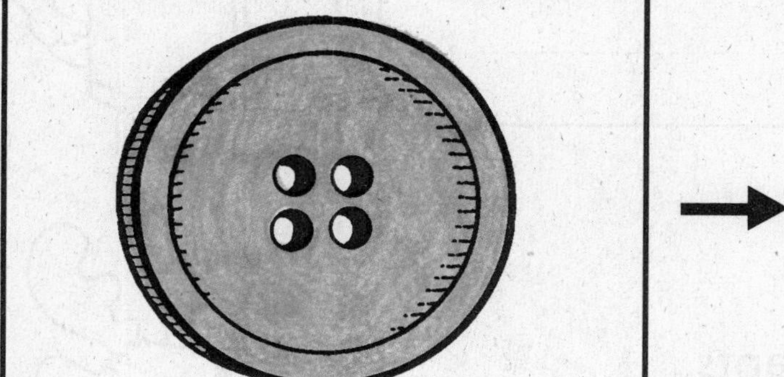

Write about some other things that the moose thought of in the story.

Name ____________________

What's Going On?

Read the sentences and look at the pictures. Then finish the sentences in your own words.

1 Mo the Moose walks in the house.
Mmmmm! There is something good in here!
It is something good to eat.

____

Mo will go ____________________
____________________________________.

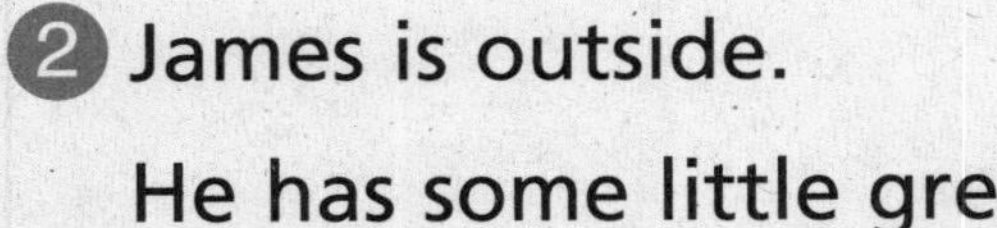

2 James is outside.
He has some little green plants.
Mo the Moose comes over.

____

Mo helps James ____________________
____________________________________.

Name ____________________

Now read these sentences and look at the pictures. Finish the sentences in your own words.

3 Mom likes to make good things to eat.
Now Mom is going out.
She is going to see Mo.

____

Mom will take Mo some ____________________
____________________.

4 Mo and James are doing something for Mom. Here are some things they have.

Write a sentence to tell what they will do.

____

____

Name

Baby Moose Has Fun

rope	tube
home	go
cone	cute

Finish each sentence by writing a word from the box in the puzzle.

1. Baby Moose is little and _____.
2. He likes the _____.
3. Big Moose helps Baby Moose _____ fast.
4. The tube has a long _____.
5. After a time Big Moose said, "We will go _____ now."
6. "I want an ice cream _____," said Baby Moose.

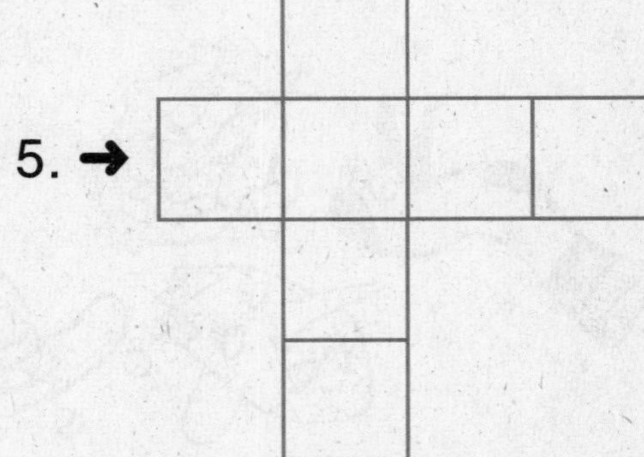

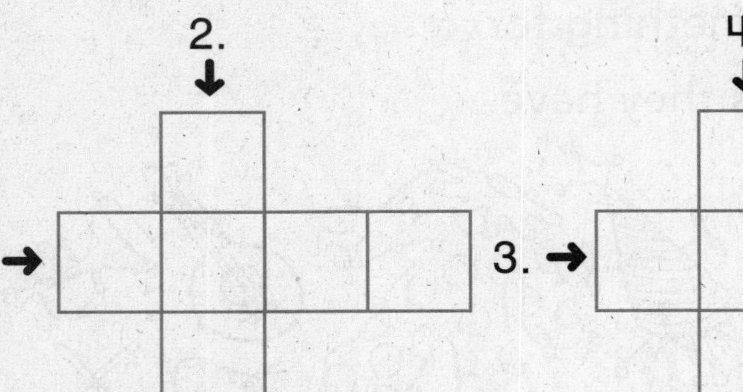

Write a sentence to tell what Big Moose might say next. Use some words from the box.

"You hope my nose will like this rose," said Little Mouse. "How good of you, Moose. I'm glad you saw my note and came back at one!"

(Fold Line)

This Is My Book

The Note

This is Little Mouse.
His cute little house
makes a good home.

One day, Little Mouse did not have one thing to eat.

"I'll have to go out," he thought.

(Fold Line)

"You do?" said Big Moose. "Why?"

"I hope your nose is OK!" said Big Moose.

"My nose is OK," said Little Mouse. "And I see why you asked me that!"

Little Mouse put a note on his door. It said:

BACK BY ONE

Big Moose saw the note. He thought it said: BROKE MY NOSE.

"That's so sad!" said Big Moose.

(Fold Line)

Then Big Moose ran home. He just had to get something for Little Mouse.

"Little Mouse will like a rose," said Big Moose.

Name ______________________________

Moose Matches

Color these pictures. Then cut out and paste the sentence that matches each picture.

Mother made this from her plants.	The moose and the boy made some of this for the show.
The moose made this from an old sock.	Give one to the moose, and he'll ask for more!

give
show
mother
ask
old

The moose had a lot of fun. Write about how you could have fun. Use some words from the box.

Name

Compound Quiz

The moose is going to be on a Compound Quiz Show! Help him write compound words using the words in the box.

any	day	dog	door	down
house	in	one	out	side
some	sun	thing	time	way

1.
2.
3.
4.
5.
6.

Now write a sentence about the moose. Use some of the compound words you wrote.

Name ______________________

Come to an Animal Party!

Invite some animal friends to a party. Choose a day and time for the party. Fill in your address. Sign your name.

____

Dear ______________________,

Please come to my animal party.

____

Day ______________________

____

Time ______________________

____

Place ______________________

____

Given by ______________________

Name ______________________________

Something's Missing

Spelling Words

go	home	bone
so	no	joke

Your Own Words

Each Spelling Word has the long **o** sound. It is the first sound in .

Write the missing letters to spell the sound. Then write the Spelling Words.

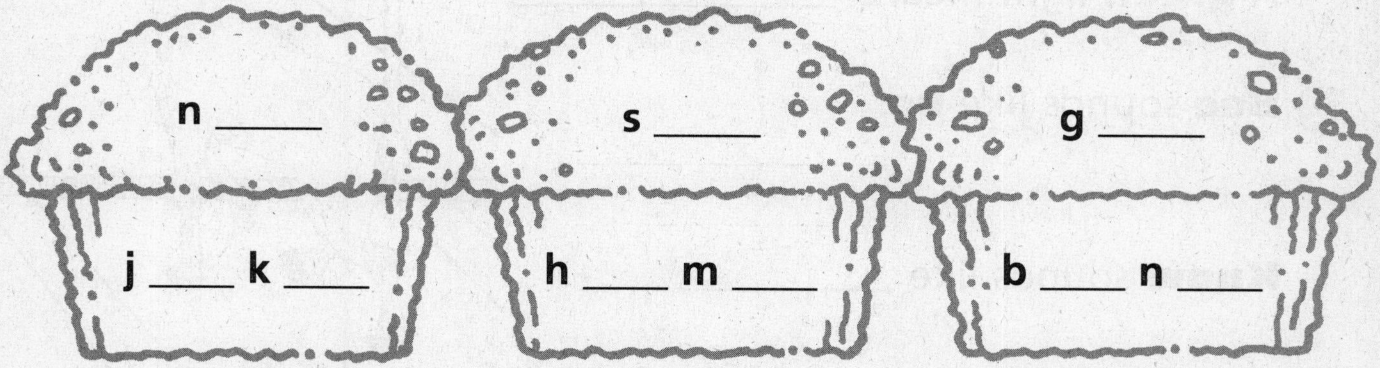

n ____ s ____ g ____

j ___ k ___ h ___ m ___ b ___ n ___

1 ______________________ 4 ______________________

2 ______________________ 5 ______________________

3 ______________________ 6 ______________________

Write the Spelling Word that begins like each picture name.

7  ______________________

8  ______________________

Name ______________________

Spelling Spree

Spelling Words		
go	home	bone
so	no	joke

Write the missing Spelling Words.

1. A red light means **stop**.

A **green** light means ______.

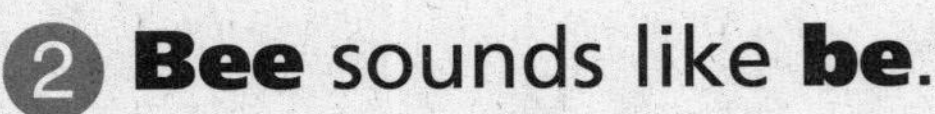

2. **Bee** sounds like **be**.

Know sounds like ______.

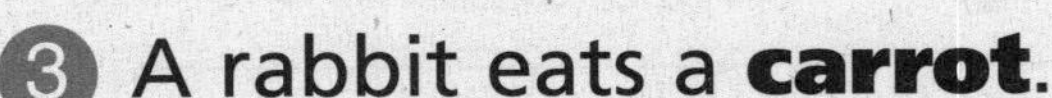

3. A rabbit eats a **carrot**.

A dog eats a ______.

Circle each Spelling Word that is wrong. Write it correctly.

4. Do not go hoem yet.

5. I will tell you a jok.

6. It is funny, soe please listen.

4 ______ 5 ______ 6 ______

Name ______________________________

Do You See More Than One?

Draw a picture for each word.

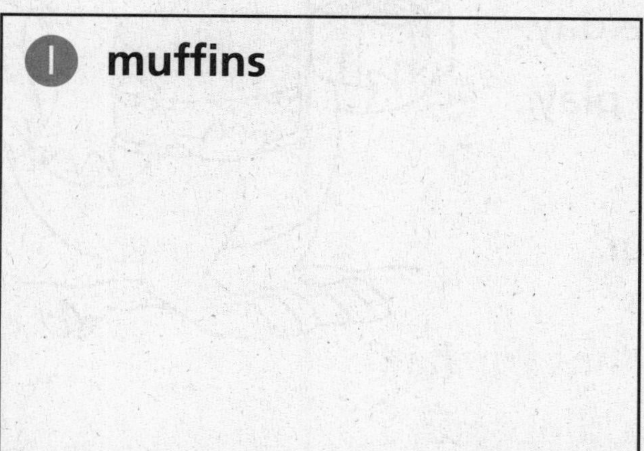

1 **muffins**

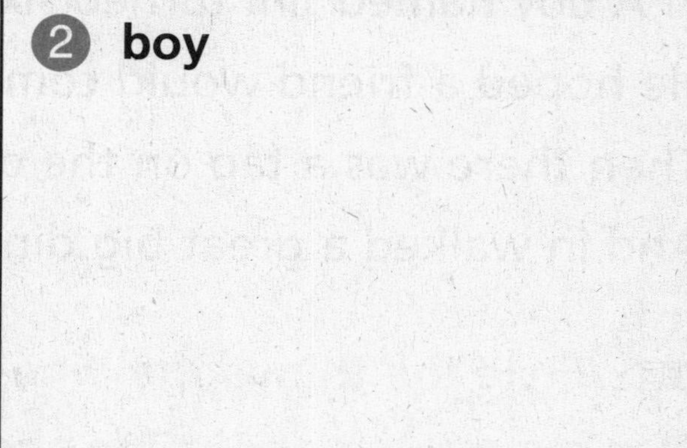

2 **boy**

Circle the naming word that goes with each picture. Then write the word.

3

sock

socks

____

5

houses

house

____

4

sheets

sheet

____

6

table

tables

____

Name ______________________

A Story Hat

Read the story starter.

A boy named Jim turned six one day.
He hoped a friend would come to play.
Then there was a tap on the door.
And in walked a great big dinosaur.

Circle the things the dinosaur has for Jim.
Plan a story hat about Jim and the dinosaur.
Show the things from the picture in your story.

Picture 1	Picture 2	Picture 3

Now make your story hat.
Check your work.

- ☐ My story hat shows what Jim and the dinosaur do.
- ☐ My pictures show the things the dinosaur gave to Jim.
- ☐ I can show my hat and tell my story.

Name ______________________

What Do You Think?

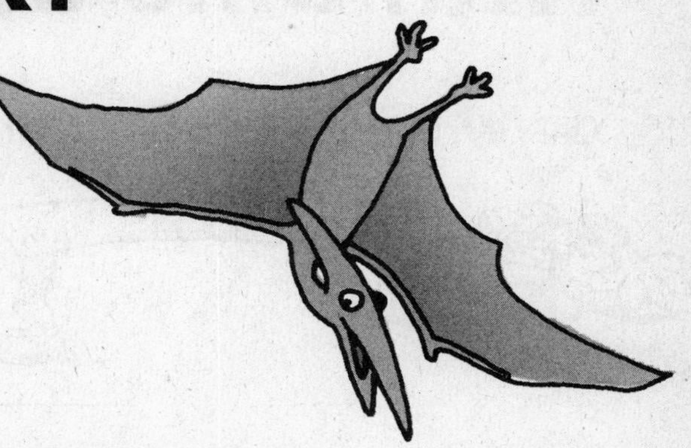

Look at this **pteranodon**. In the clue boxes, draw things that make it look special.

Clue:	Clue:	Clue:

Now tell about one of those things.

Pteranodons ______________________.

Finish this sentence.

If a pteranodon came back, it could help ______________________
______________________.

Name

With Dino and Me

needs
we
weeds
sleep
teeth

Write a word to finish each sentence.

1 Dino likes to eat ______________.

2 Dino ______________ to go for a walk.

3 Then ________ will go back to the house.

4 What big ______________ my Dino has!

5 Now Dino will go to ______________.

Write a sentence about Dino. Use a word with long **e** in your sentence.

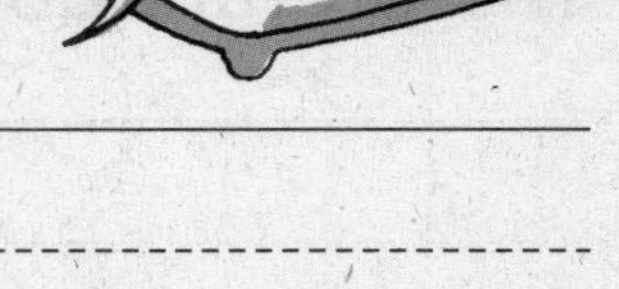

They jumped to the street.
And they said, "We'll go by **feet**!"

(Fold Line)

This Is My Book

Three Baby Geese

Three baby geese
walked down the street.

They jumped in a jeep.
Then it picked up speed!

(Fold Line)

The jeep went **beep**!
The geese said **peep**!

Name ______________________________

Al Goes to Work

Al is an allosaurus. Read the story about him and look at his picture here and on the next page. Then finish the sentences.

It is time for Al to go to work. He always stops on the way. This time he stops to read about a new show.

It will take Al a long time to get to work. When he gets there, he will build something new.

1 Al will go ______________________________.

2 At work Al will ______________________________.

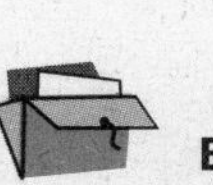

Now draw a line to show where Al should go. At the end of the line, draw a picture of what Al will build.

Name

Dinosaur Concentration

Cut out the cards. Use them to play Dinosaur Concentration with a partner. Keep the cards in an envelope to play another day!

for	four	to	two
son	sun	would	wood
eight	ate	new	knew
one	won	there	their
be	bee	sea	see

Name ______________________

Tricky Triceratops

Write about what you see in this picture. Describe it from side to side. Use the words in the box.

triceratops
slide
swings
seesaw
rings

Name

Feed the Dinosaurs

Spelling Words		
we	be	see
need	tree	me

Your Own Words

Each Spelling Word has the long **e** sound.
It is the first sound in  .

Write each Spelling Word under the matching spelling for the long e sound.

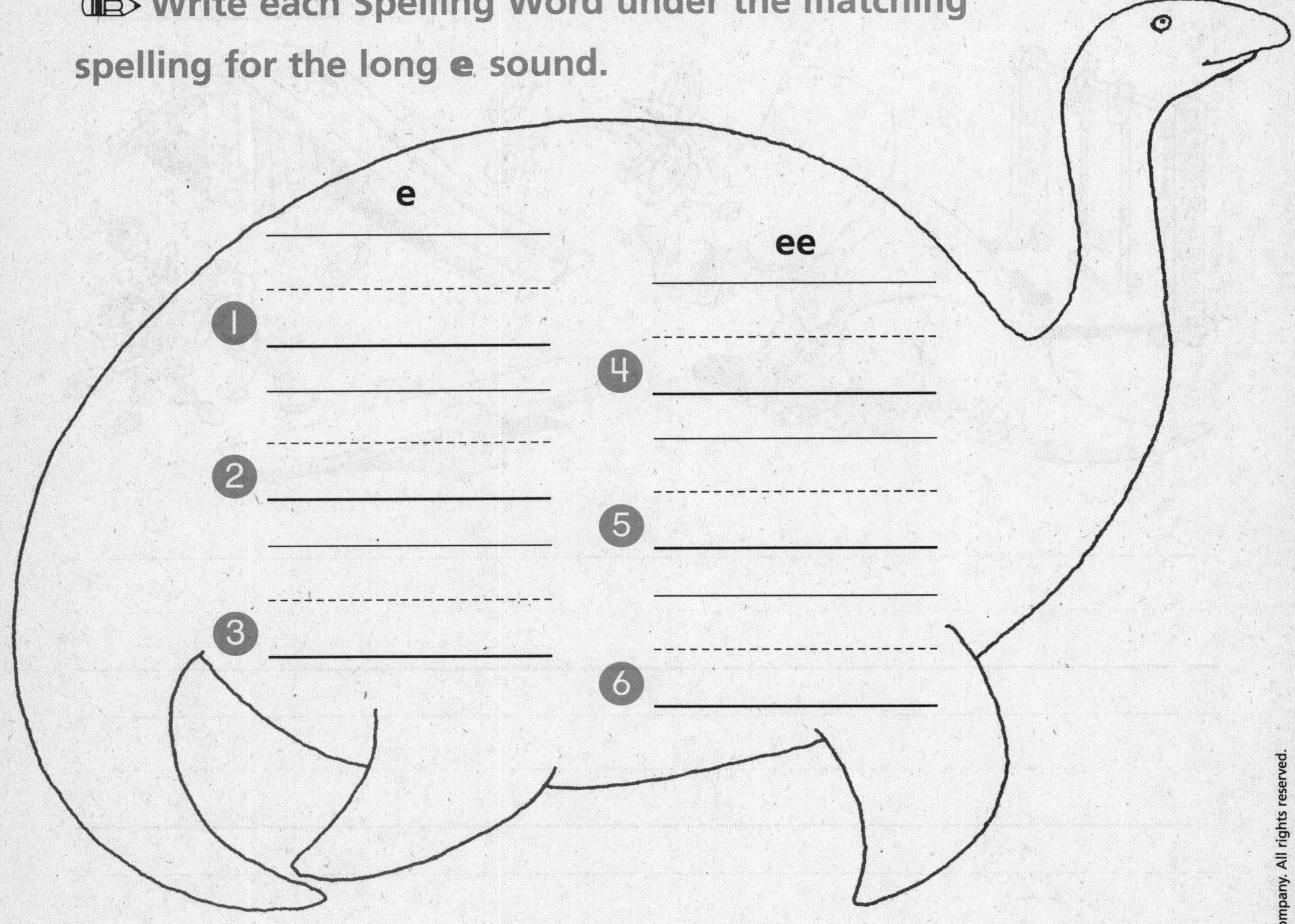

e

1

2

3

ee

4

5

6

Write the Spelling Word that begins like each picture name.

Name ______________________

Spelling Spree

Spelling Words		
we	be	see
need	tree	me

Write the letter for each clue.
Make Spelling Words.

1 I am in **bad** but not in **pad**.
2 I am in **get** but not in **got**.

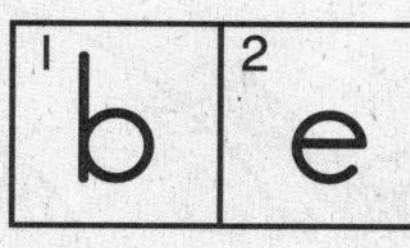

3 I am in **win** but not in **pin**.
4 I am in **set** but not in **sit**.

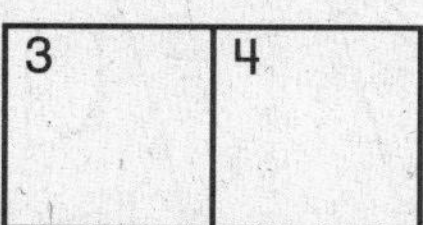

5 I am in **nut** but not in **cut**.
6 I am in **pen** but not in **pan**.
7 I am in **let** but not in **lot**.
8 I am in **dip** but not in **tip**.

5	6	7	8

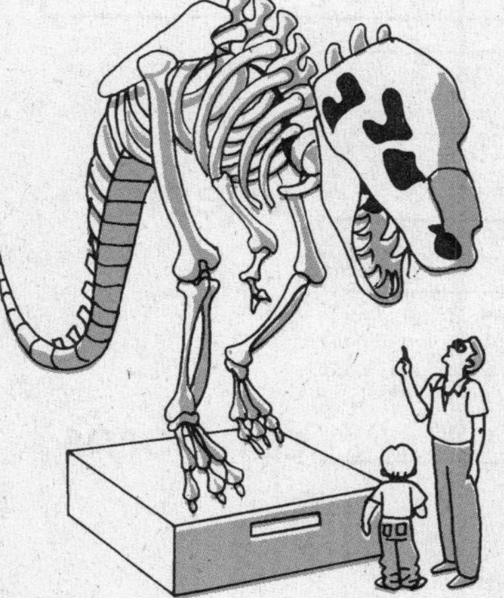

Circle four Spelling Words that are wrong.
Write each word correctly.

Dear Diary,

I went to se some dinosaurs. Dad came with mea. We stood next to one dinosaur. It was as tall as a tre.

I wonder if dinosaurs will ever bee back?

9 ____________ 10 ____________ 11 ____________ 12 ____________

Name

Big and Beautiful!

round	furry
little	loud
two	big

Use words from the box that best tell about the picture. Write the words.

1 ______ dinosaur

2 ______ baby

3 ______ wheels

4 ______ car horns

Now write a sentence about the picture. Use a word from the box.

Name ______________________________

A Great Dream

Circle a word to finish each sentence, and draw a picture.

Draw the dream's ending on another sheet of paper.

1. I went to sleep. I ____ that my parents went out.

   dreamt **home** **father**

2. I found my brother putting ____ on the plants and on the cat!

   water **room** **parents**

3. My other brother asked to play with things in my ____.

   father **room** **found**

4. Then my father came ____ with a big, big fish.

   dreamt **brother** **home**

Name

Little George

Write or draw what happened in the story.

At the Beginning

In the Middle

At the End

Name ____________________

Two Stories–Alike or Different?

Look through the two stories. Draw two things that are alike in both stories and two things that are different.

There's an Alligator Under My Bed

Alike

George Shrinks

Name

Sea Dreams

Read the words in the box. Then help George finish each picture name.

goat	leaf	peach	crow	boat

l ___ ___ f

p ___ ___ c h

g ___ ___ t

c r ___ ___

b ___ ___ t

"It's a good thing I have
some soap!" said Dean.

(Fold Line)

This Is My Book

Beat the Heat

"Let's load our boat," said Dean.

"Then we can row down
the stream," said Joan.

(Fold Line)

"Who needs the beach?" said Joan.
"We can soak in the boat!"

"What a neat way to
beat the heat!" said Dean.

(Fold Line)

"Here – have a peach!"

"No time to eat," said Joan.
"We have a leak."

(Fold Line)

"When we reach the beach
we can jump in."

Name ______________________

Dear George

Help George read the note from his mother.
Finish each sentence with the correct word.

water	brother	room	play	home

Dear George,

I found the cat. Will you put some ______________ in her pan? Give your ______________ his snack. Your father will be ______________ at six. There is something new for you to ______________ with. Look for it in your ______________.

Love,
Mother

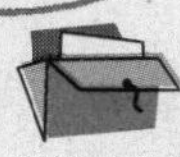

Connect the dots to see the surprise for George.

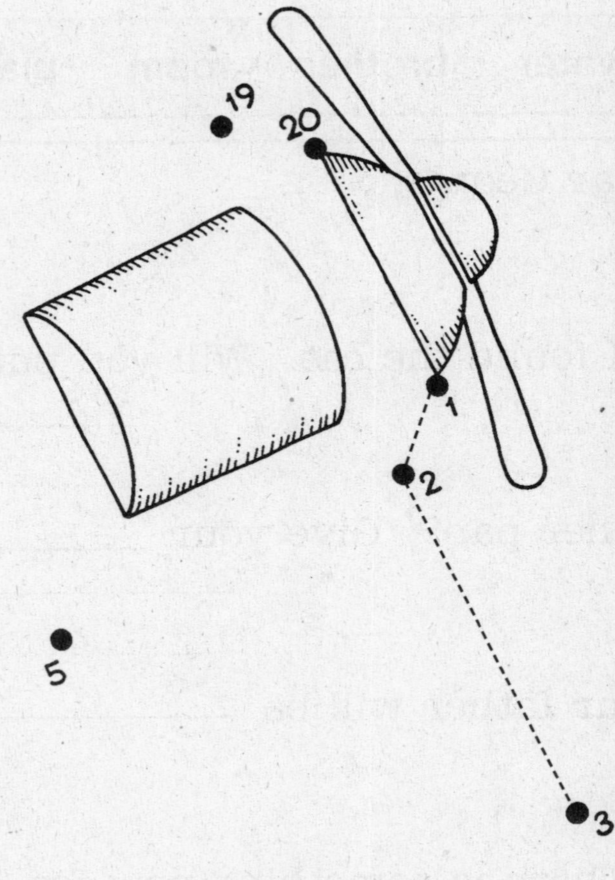

Tell what George found in his room.

Name ______________________

Where Is George?

Circle the word to finish each sentence. Cut out the boxes and paste them on separate sheets of paper. Draw a picture for each page and make a book.

Where Is George?	Look _____. close closely 1
George is so little. His dog _____ walked over him. nearly near 2	The dog went WOOF very _____. loud loudly 3
George thought _____. quick quickly 4	He hid _____ in back of a big plant. safely safe 5

Name ______________________________

Breakfast Treats

What would you like to have for breakfast? Draw a picture.

Write some describing words to tell about your breakfast.

It looks ______________________________.

It tastes ______________________________.

It smells ______________________________.

It feels ______________________________.

It sounds ______________________________.

Name

Special Delivery

Spelling Words		
eat	each	seat
clean	read	mean
Your Own Words		

Each Spelling Word has the long **e** sound.
It has the first sound in .

Find out what George got in the mail.
Color each part that has a word with the  sound.

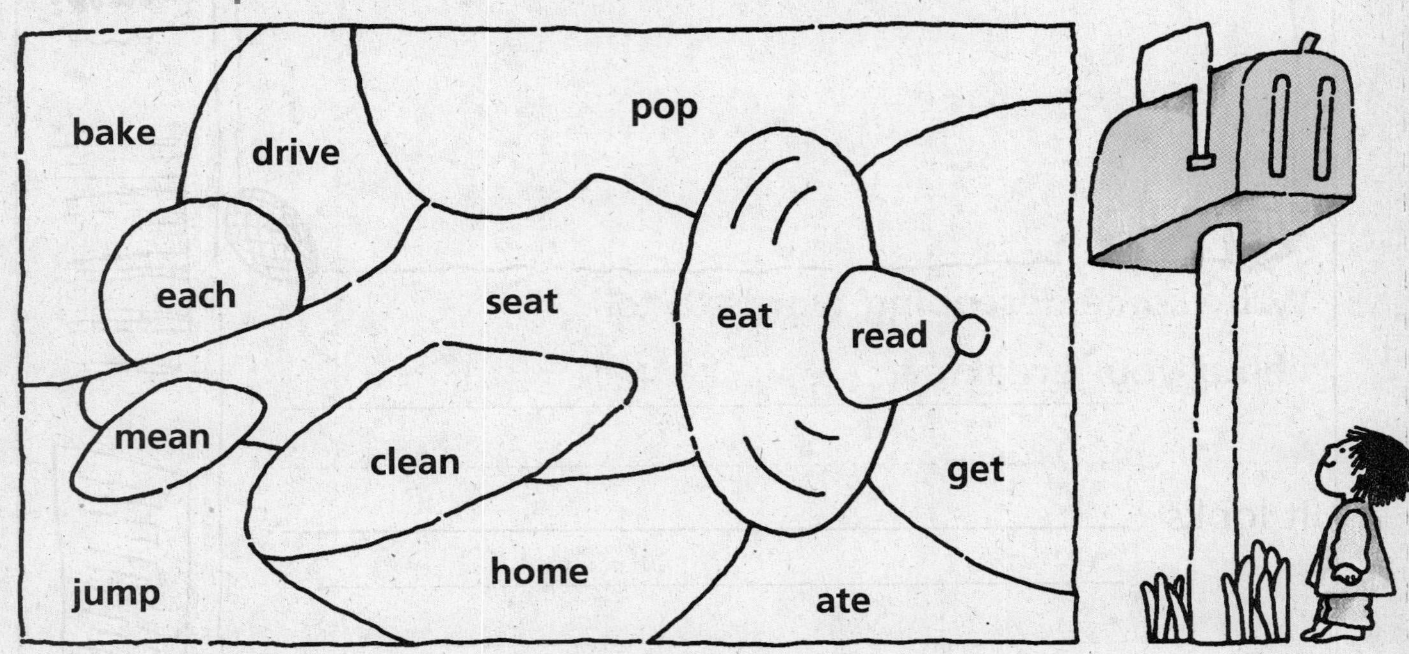

Write the Spelling Words from the parts you colored.

1 ________ 3 ________ 5 ________

2 ________ 4 ________ 6 ________

Draw a line under the letters that spell the  sound in each word you wrote.

Name

Spelling Spree

Spelling Words		
eat	each	seat
clean	read	mean

Write the missing Spelling Words.

1. You lie in a bed.
   You sit in a ____.
2. You watch a movie.
   You ____ a book.
3. You drink milk.
   You ____ cheese.

Circle three Spelling Words that are wrong. Write each word correctly.

Lunch List

- [x] Make sure my hands are cleen.
- [x] Then eat lunch.
- [ ] Wash eche dish in the sink.
- [ ] Do not be meen to my sister.

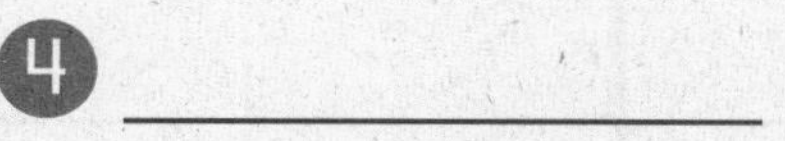

4. ____  5. ____ 6. ____

Name

Describe It!

How does each thing taste, smell, or feel? Write a word from the airplane.

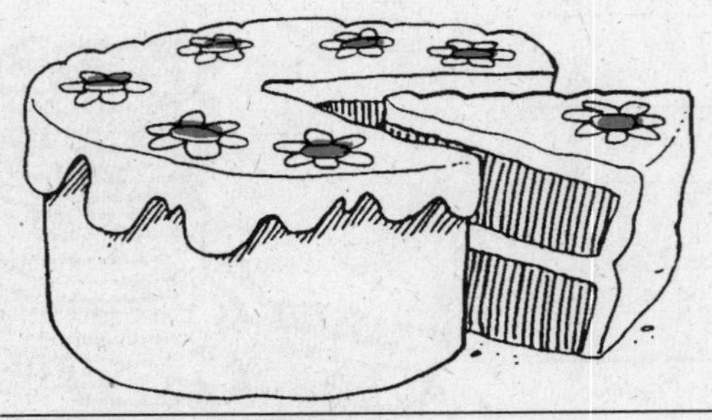

1 ______

3 ______

2 ______

4 ______

Now write your own sentence. Use one of the words you wrote.

Name

What's It Like?

What do you want to tell about? Draw or write your idea in the big circle. Then write describing words about it in the other circles.

Name

Take Another Look

Revising Checklist

Ask yourself these questions about your description.

- ☐ Do I use words that tell how it looks, feels, tastes, sounds, or smells?
- ☐ Do I tell enough so that someone can picture it?

Things I want to add to my description

Questions to Ask My Writing Partner

- Can you picture what I am describing?
- Is there anything that is not clear?
- Is there anything I should add?
- What do you like best about my description?

Katelyn Mailk
Name

Playing with Possum

Write words from the box to finish what Possum is saying.

bring	because
mighty	friend
find	

I am Possum. I am sad 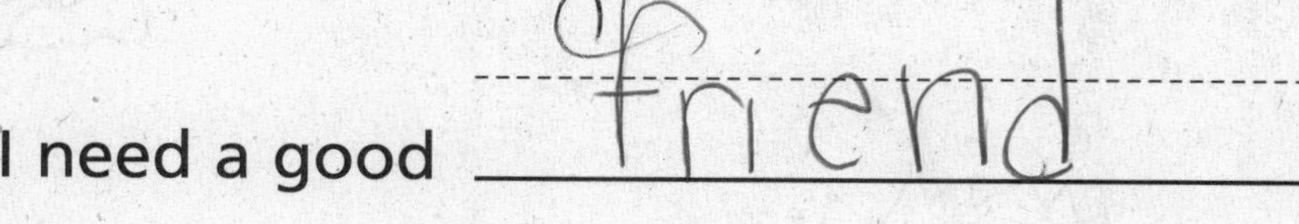 ________

I need a good ________. Can you help me

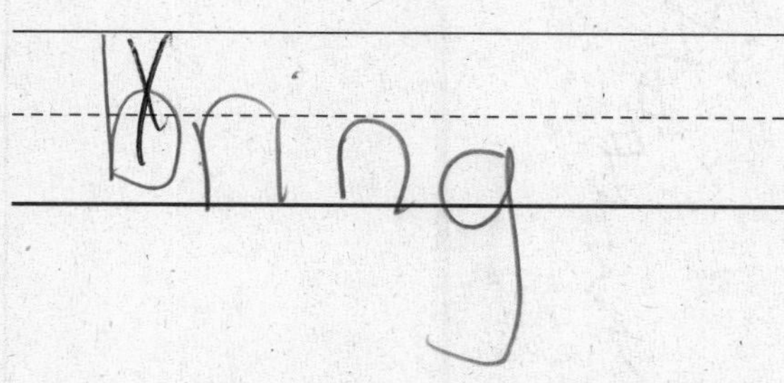

________ some friends?

In the morning, I will have a tug of war with my brothers.

They are big and 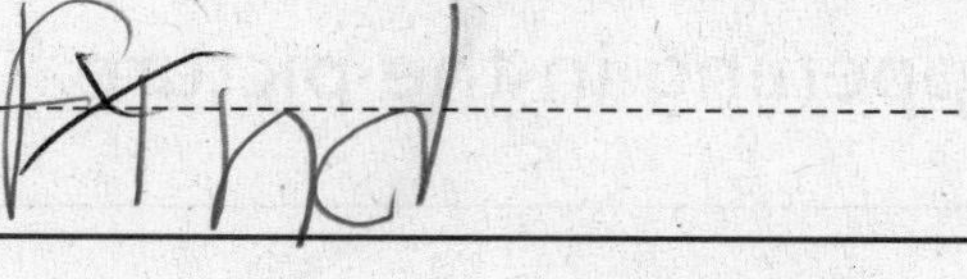 ________, but I am just

little. I need friends to help me. Come and

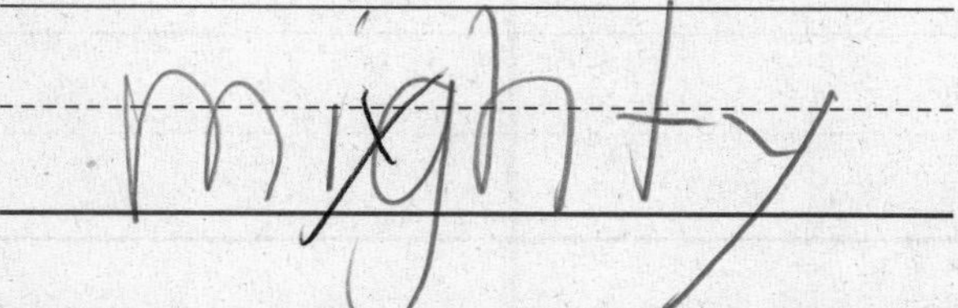

________ others with you.

The tug of war will start at 10:00 in the morning.

Name

Tug. Tug. Who Wins?

Finish the picture to show the tug of war.
Draw the animals in the right places.

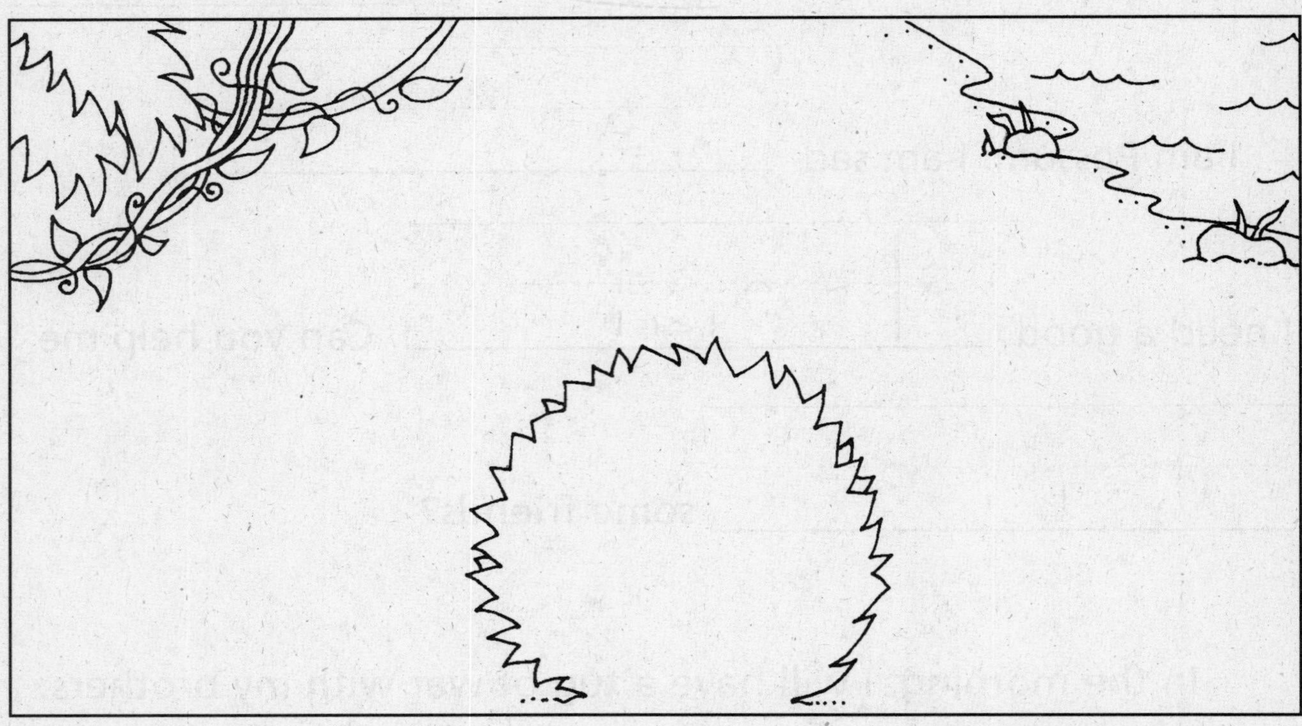

Tell what is happening in the picture.

Name ______________________________

A Bigger Bed for Baby

✂ Cut out and paste the pictures to show what happens or why it happens.

Cause	What Happens
PASTE HERE	The bed is too little.
Big Dad sits on the little bed.	PASTE HERE
The hammer hits Big Dad.	PASTE HERE
It is time for bed.	PASTE HERE

Name ______________________________

Play Time

Complete each sentence about Hal the hippo.

1. It is late, but Hal likes to ______________.
   plate play

2. So Hal makes things out of ______________.
   clay clap

3. He plays with some ______________.
   pat paints

4. And he makes his ______________ go very fast.
   train tray

Cut out only the toys Hal played with. Paste them on the back of this page to help Hal clean up.

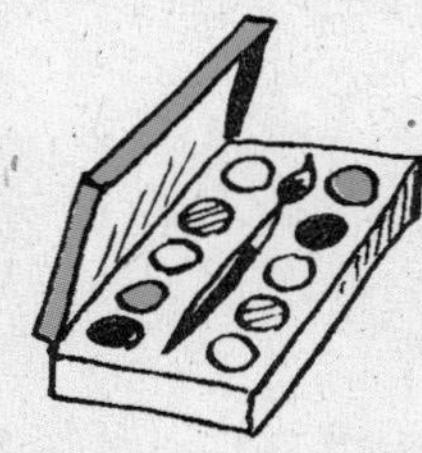

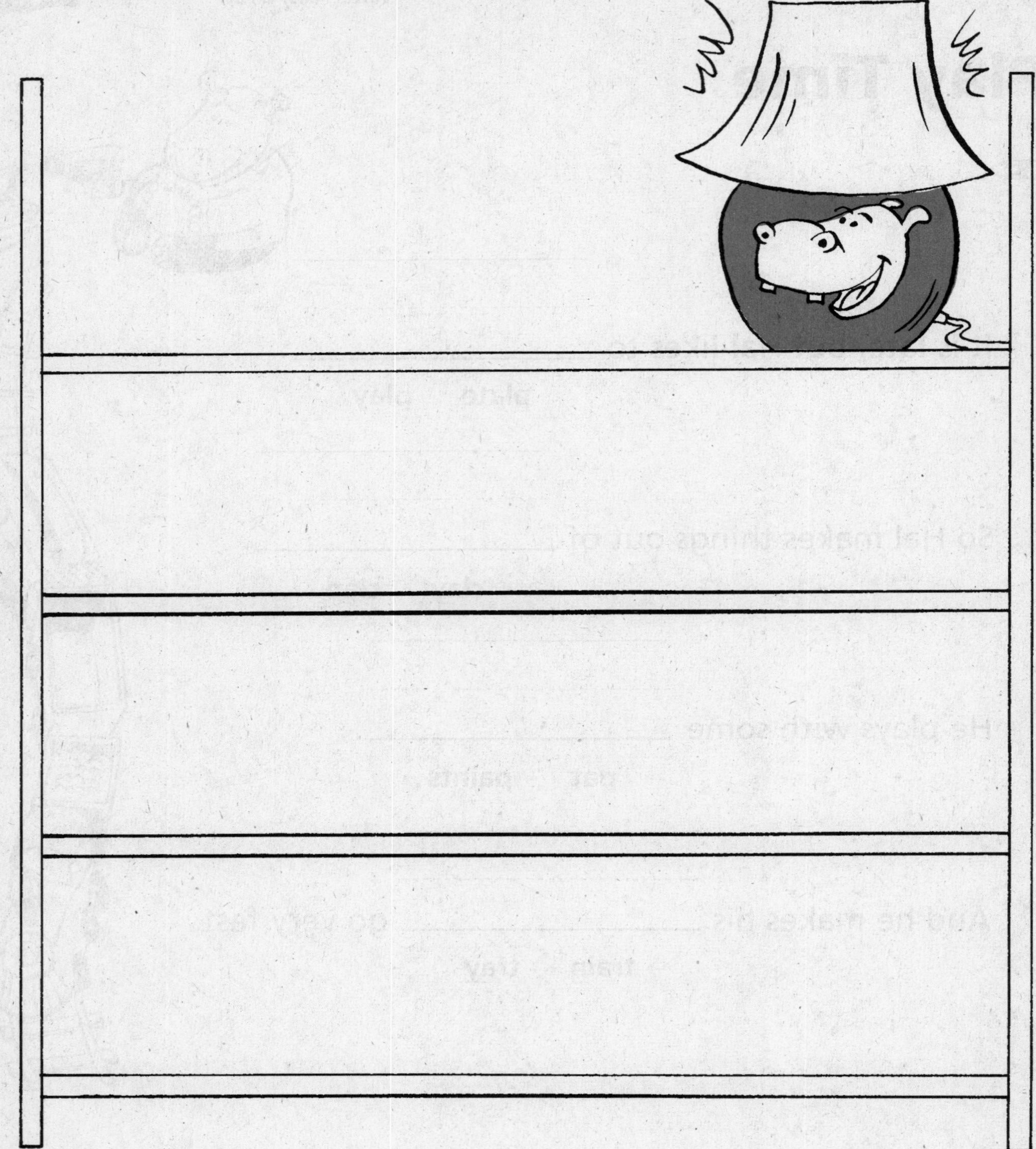

"It may be a play day after all!" said Gail. And she went on her way.

(Fold Line)

This Is My Book

Rain, Rain, Go Away!

"It's a gray day," said Gail the Snail. "We cannot go out to play."

"Rain, rain, do not stay.
Can't you see we like to play?"

(Fold Line)

The rain did stop. And out
came a ray of sun!

Name ______________________

Off and Running

Write the words to finish the story.

Then color the pictures.

1 The sun is up, and it is ______________.

morning mother

2 They are about to ______________.

sleep start

3 Some ______________ their little brothers.

big bring

4 They ______________ something to eat.

find fish

They are glad because their friend wins!

Name

Hippo at Play

Tell what Hippo did. Add **ed** to the words to finish the sentences. What else must you add?

1 Hippo ________________.
skip

2 Hippo ________________.
trip

3 Hippo ________________.
hop

4 Hippo ________________.
slip

5 Hippo ________________.
flip

6 Hippo ________________.
flop

Name ______________________________

The Great Contest

Make up a story about a contest like the one in The Tug of War.

Who is the
fairest
smartest
fastest
funniest
one of all?

What will the contest be about?

____

Who is the ______________________________ one of all?

Draw or write your ideas for your story. Tell who will be in your story and what will happen.

Name

Tug Away

Each Spelling Word has the long **a** sound. It is the first sound in a.

Spelling Words		
day	play	way
may	say	stay

Your Own Words

Write the missing letters to spell the sound. Then write each Spelling Word.

1 pl ay
may

3 d ay
day

5 m ay
way

2 st ay
say

4 s ay
day

6 w ay
day

Write the Spelling Word that begins like each picture name.

7

8

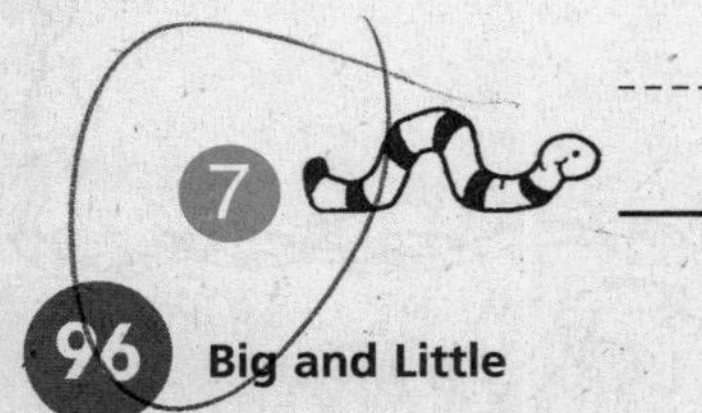

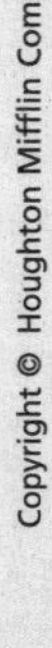

Name

Spelling Spree

Spelling Words		
day	play	way
may	say	stay

Write the Spelling Word for each clue.

1 **not** work

2 **not** leave

3 **not** night

Circle three Spelling Words that are wrong. Write each word correctly.

Dear Elephant and Hippo,
Listen to what I have to sai.
I mae be little, but I am strong.
Is there a wa we can still play?

4 ______ 5 ______ 6 ______

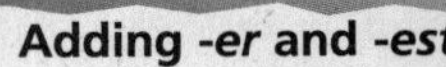

Name

How Are They Different?

Add **er** or **est** on the lines to make new words.

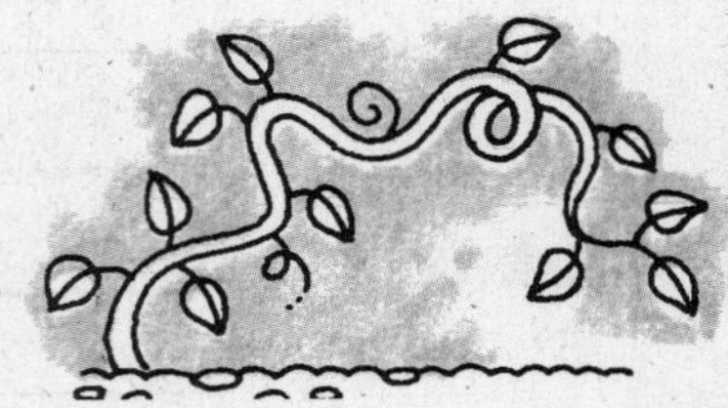

1 long

2 long ______

3 long ______

4 deep

5 deep ______

6 deep ______

Write a sentence about the picture below. Use the word **taller** or **tallest** in your sentence.

7 ______

Name

Making a Survival Kit

Think of the things you do at home or at school. If you were very small, like George in **George Shrinks**, how would you do them? What things would you want to have in your kit?

Make the survival kit you would use.

Check your work.

- ☐ I made a sentence about being very small.
- ☐ I made pictures of things in my kit and how I use them.
- ☐ I can tell why I picked the things in my kit.

Name ______________________________

Whose Shoes?

Read and follow the directions.

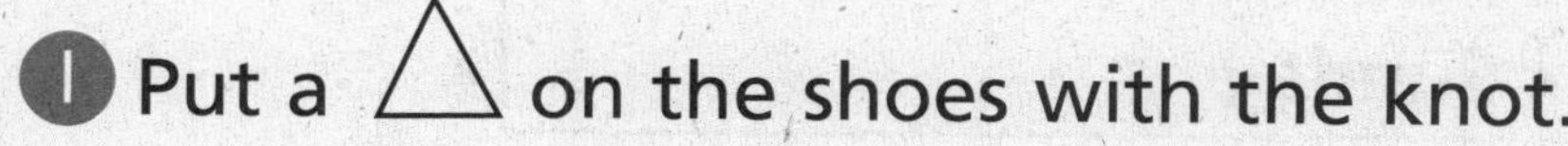

1 Put a △ on the shoes with the knot.

2 Put an **X** on the shoes that are in a tangle.

3 Put a ○ on the child who is barefoot.

Finish the sentence. Draw a picture.

I wore my ____________________ shoes to ____________________.

Name

Shoes for Every Day

Monday	Tuesday	Wednesday	Thursday
Friday	Saturday	Sunday	

Write the name of the day. Draw the shoes for each day in the story.

Monday

T

W

T

F

S

S

Name

Getting Started

What favorite thing are you going to write about? Write your idea in the center circle. Then write what you want to say about it in the other circles.

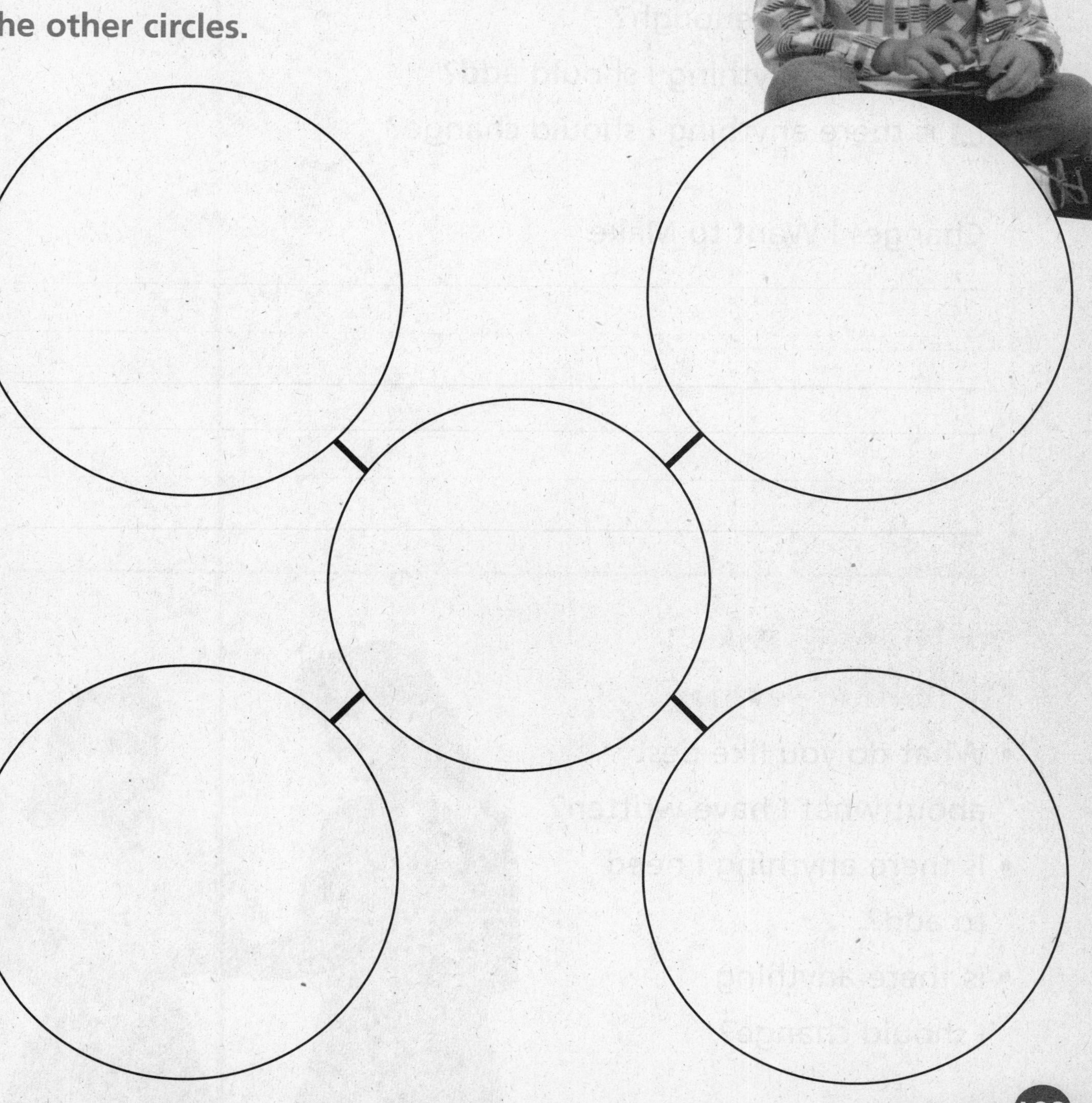

Name

Take Another Look

Revising Checklist

Answer these questions about what you have done.

- ❑ Have I told enough?
- ❑ Is there anything I should add?
- ❑ Is there anything I should change?

Changes I Want to Make

Questions to Ask My Writing Partner

- What do you like best about what I have written?
- Is there anything I need to add?
- Is there anything I should change?

Name

What Happens?

In the box, write the problem Tapidou has in **The Tug of War**. In the oval, draw how Tapidou solved the problem.

Character
Tapidou

Problem

Solution

Name

Choco's Path

Help Choco find Mrs. Bear. Follow the path of words that have long **i** spelled **y**.

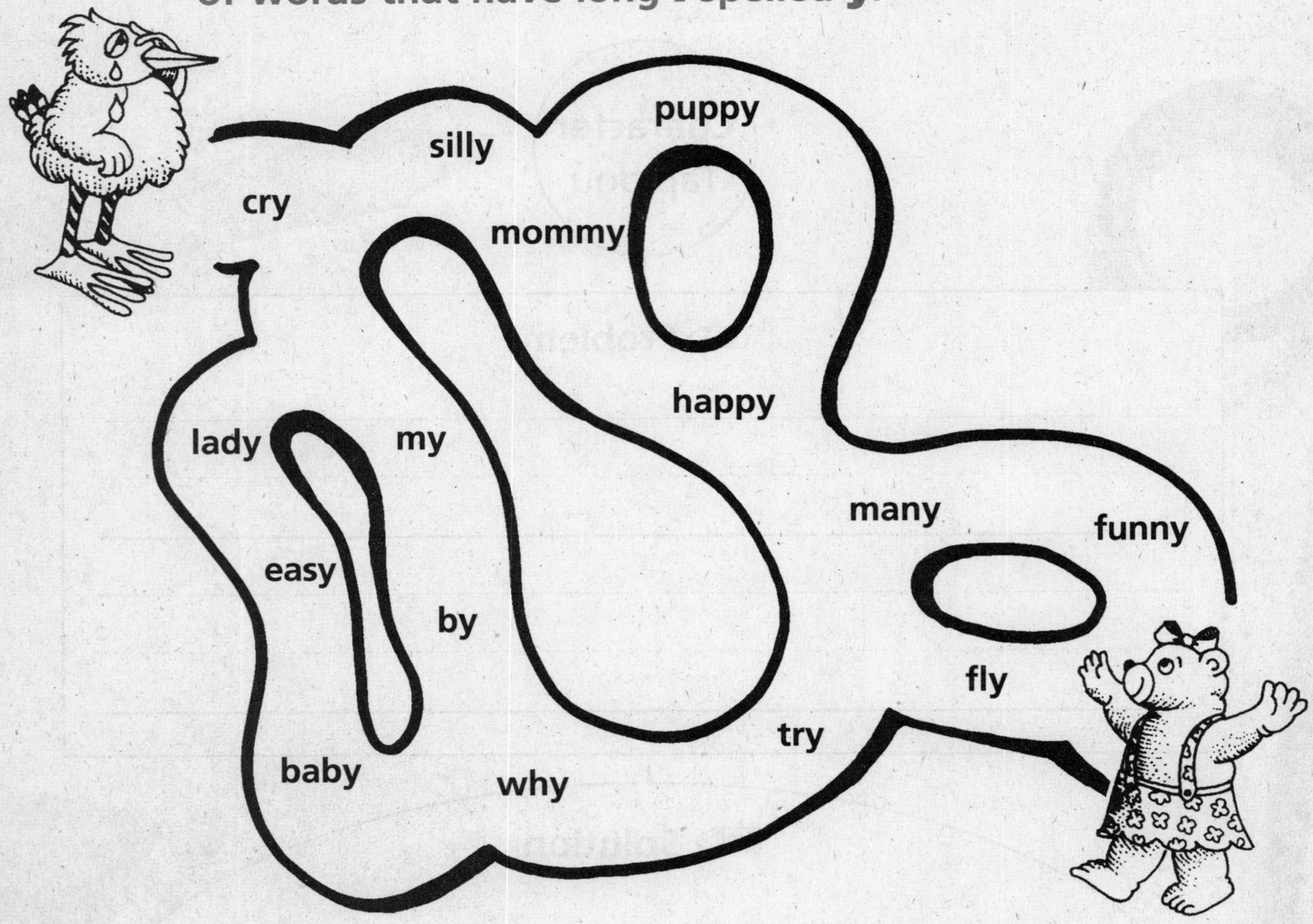

cry
silly
puppy
mommy
happy
lady
my
easy
by
many
funny
fly
try
baby
why

Write a word from the paths to finish each sentence.

1 Choco is not ________________.

2 He cries, "I want ________________ mother!"

"You are **not** a silly little puppy," said his mommy. "You **look** more like a silly little piggy!"

(Fold Line)

This Is My Book

A puppy looked up and saw a fly go by in the sky.

"I can fly, too!" said the puppy.

"You are a silly little puppy,"

said his mommy.

(Fold Line)

"I am not silly," said the puppy.

He ran. He jumped.

Down he came into the mud.

Name ______________________

Finding a Mother

Cut out and paste the sentences in order to tell about **A Mother for Choco**. Draw pictures to go with them.

Next, he asked Mrs. Walrus, "Are you my mother?"

"No," she said. "Get out of here!"

First, Choco asked Mrs. Giraffe, "Are you my mother?"

"No," she said, as she gave him a pat on the back.

So Choco lived with Mrs. Bear and her other children. He had found a mother.

Choco said, "I'll never find my mother!"

"Would you like to come home with me?" Mrs. Bear asked. "Then we would be together."

Name ______________________________

In Order

A B C D E F G H I J K L M N O P Q R S T U V W X Y Z

Write the missing letters.

a b c d ____ f g ____ ____ ____ k ____

____ ____ o p q r s t ____ v ____ x y z

Cut out the words and put them in ABC order. Paste them on paper and draw pictures to show their meanings.

house	**children**	**tree**
sun	**baby**	**eat**

Name ______________________

First, Next, and Last

My Story

Write sentences to tell about each picture. Tell what happened **first**, what happened **next**, and what happened **last**.

Name

Try This!

Each Spelling Word has the long **i** sound. It is the first sound in .

Draw a line from dot to dot to find a letter that spells the sound. Then draw a line under this letter in each word.

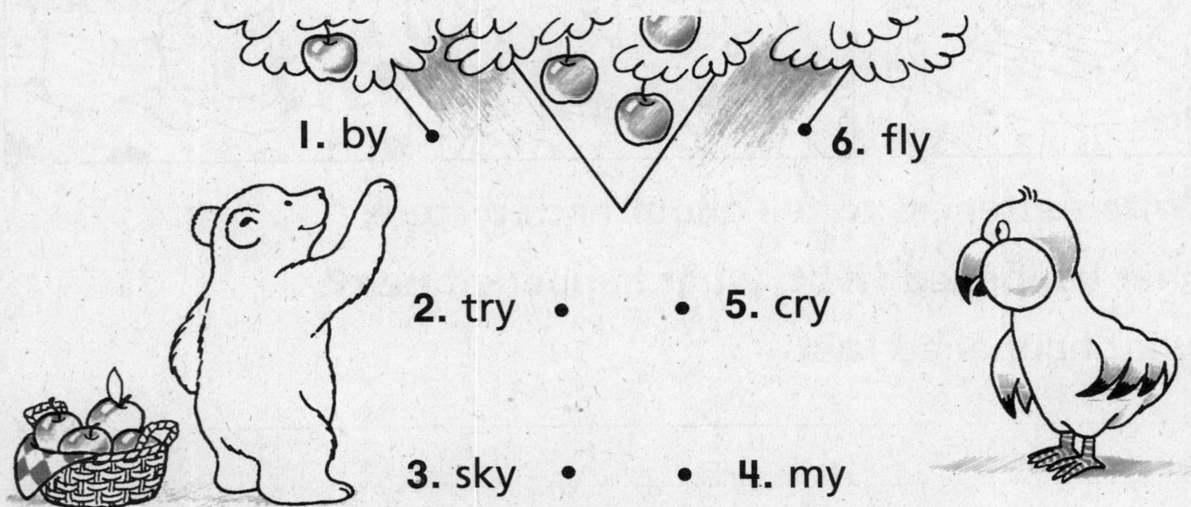

Write the Spelling Word that begins like each picture name.

1 ______

2 ______

3 ______

4 ______

5 ______

6 ______

Name

Spelling Spree

Spelling Words		
my	by	fly
cry	try	sky

Write the Spelling Word for each clue.

1. what birds do
2. where stars shine
3. a sad sound

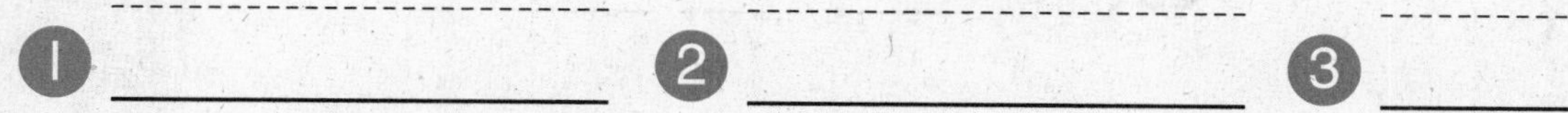

1 ________ 2 ________ 3 ________

Circle three Spelling Words that are wrong. Write each word correctly.

Mrs. Bear's Pie Store

Calling all birds!
Fly in and taste mye pie.
I sell it bi the slice.
Please tri some today.

4 ________ 5 ________ 6 ________

Name

Animal Match

Match the pictures and the action words. Write each action word.

fly

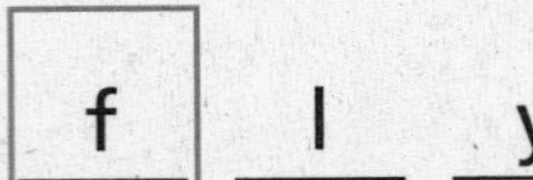

eat

swim

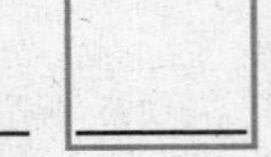

sit

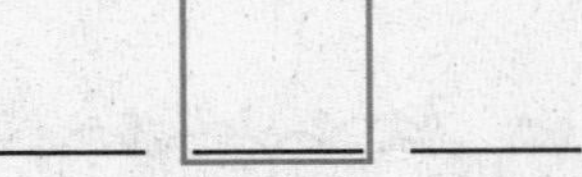

roll

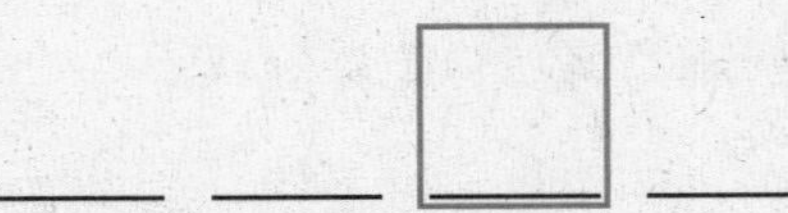

play

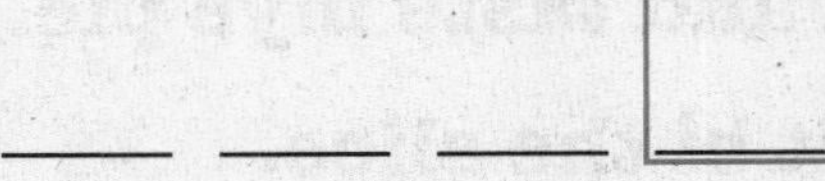

Write the letters from the boxes to answer the question.

What did Choco find? a ______________________

Name ______________________

Let's Sew

Write the word in the puzzle for each clue.

afraid	head
material	needle
school	throw
turn	

Down

1. I like to read after ___ every day.
2. I'm ___ you are right. I can't find it.
3. I can ___ my vest inside out.
4. You make a hat for your ___.

Across

5. Don't ___ out that coat!
6. A coat is made out of ___.
7. You need a ___ to make a dress.

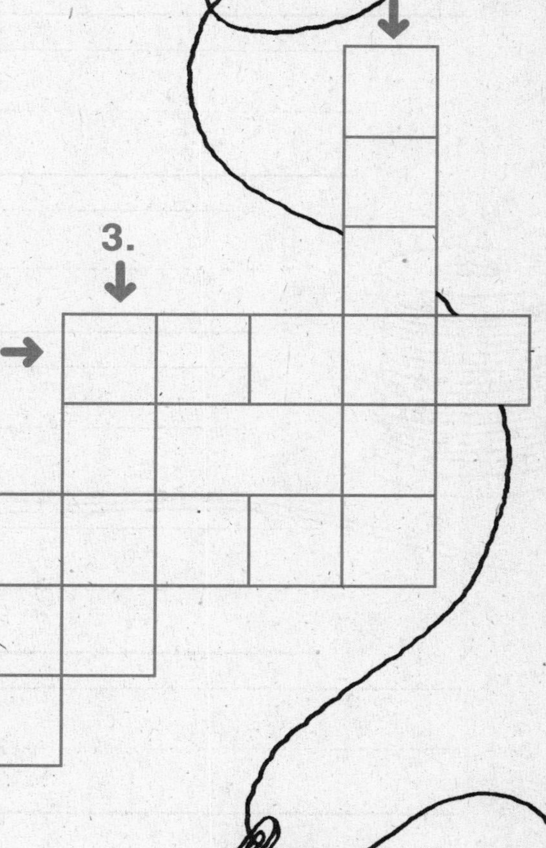

What would you like to make with material?

____

____

Name

Finish Joseph's Story

Write in order what Grandpa made.
(The words in the box may help you.)

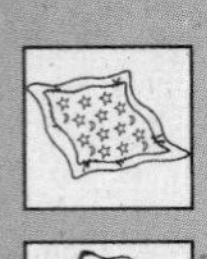 blanket

 tie

 handkerchief

 vest

 jacket

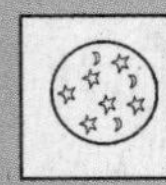 button

Grandpa made a . . .

1

2

3

4

5

6

What did Joseph make from nothing?

Now use this page to tell the story!

Name

Joseph's Blanket

Cut out the things Grandpa made from the blanket.
Paste them in the order that they were made.

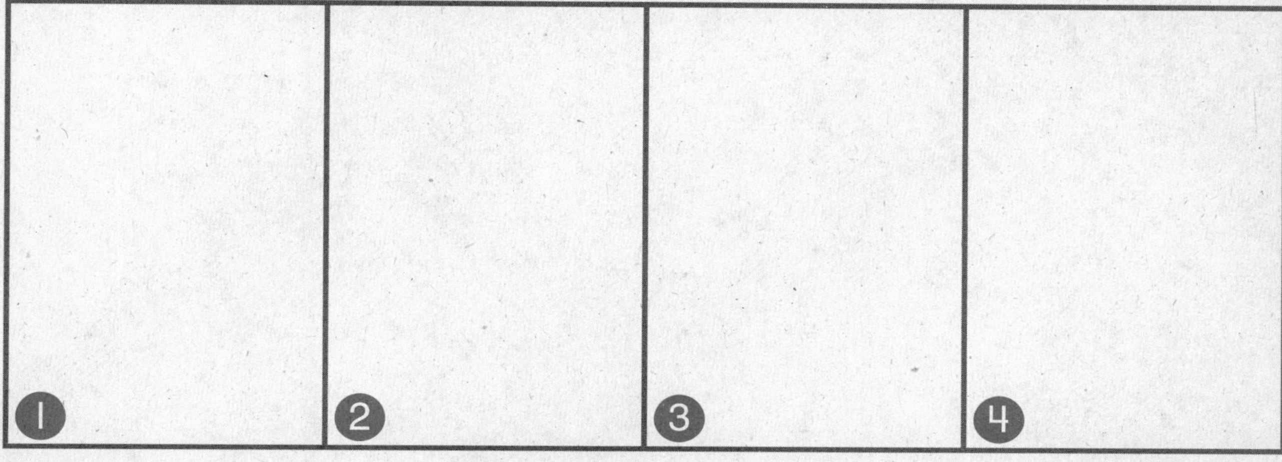

Write a sentence about the last thing Grandpa made.

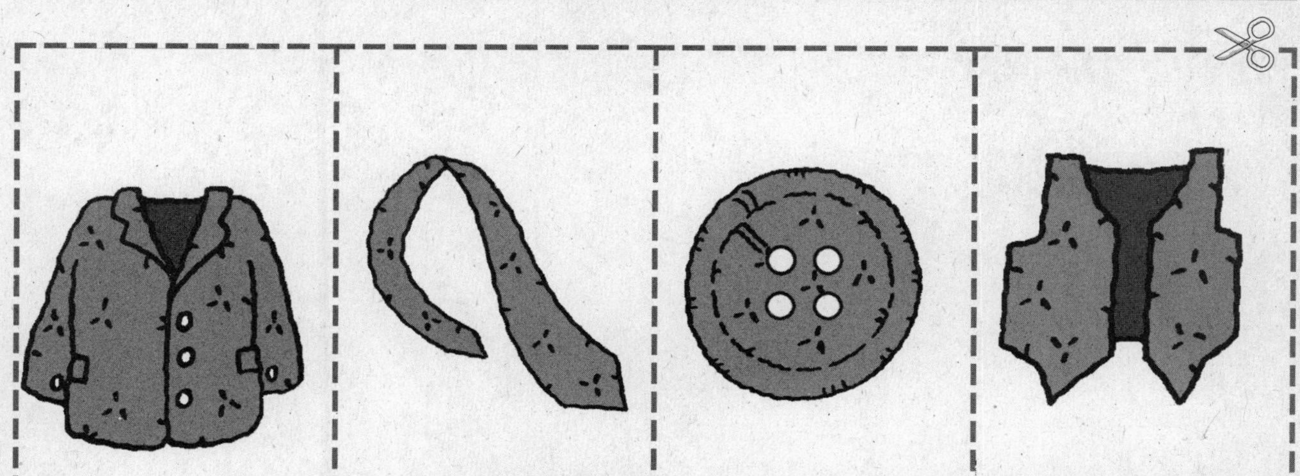

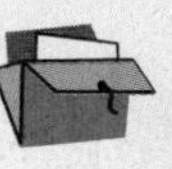

Name ______________________

A Few Clues for You, Too!

Grandpa has some riddles about Joseph. Write the answers for him.

1. Joseph did this. The vest did not. (Fold)
   - good ______
   - grew ______
   - glue ______

2. Look! It will rain! Joseph will put this on his foot. (Fold)
   - blue ______
   - beat ______
   - boot ______

3. Joseph eats with this. It helps him eat his soup. (Fold)
   - stood ______
   - spoon ______
   - stew ______

4. When Joseph goes to school, he can read this. (Fold)
   - book ______
   - brook ______
   - broom ______

Cut and fold each riddle. Share them with your family.

But I do!

(Fold Line)

This Is My Book

A True Stew Story

Every day Lou's mother
cooks him stew to bring to school.

And every day Lou would like
to shoot his stew to the moon!

(Fold Line)

Is stew good food?
"I don't like it," says Lou.

Name

Little Owl Hoots

Read the story. Then write about what Little Owl does at school the next day.

Little Owl was not happy. He could throw a leaf with his beak. But he could not hoot.

Every day at school, Mrs. Robin asked him to hoot. "I am afraid I can't," said Little Owl.

"How do you hoot?" Little Owl asked his mother. "Turn your head and look up at the moon. Do you see the Man-in-the-Moon?"

"Who?" asked Little Owl. "Who? Who? Whooo?"

"Little Owl," said Mother Owl, "that is right!"

"GOOD!" said Little Owl. "Now I can hoot."

The next day at school,

Name ____________________

Dear Mia

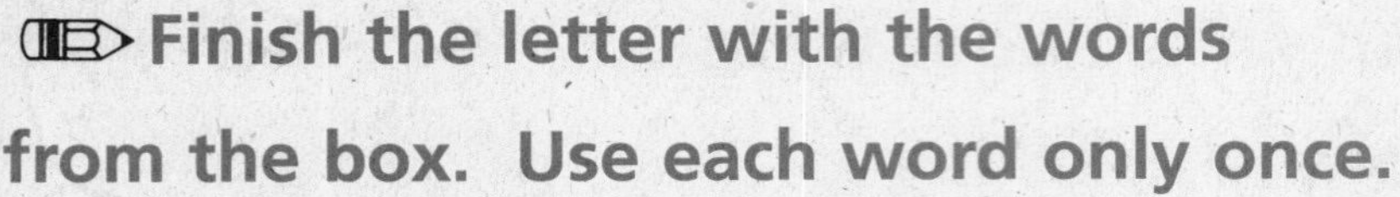

Finish the letter with the words from the box. Use each word only once.

My	His
her	your

Dear Mia,

I just moved into a new home. ____________ room is so big. You would like it. You would have space for all of ____________ toys.

My mother likes our new home. She found lots of blue material to make things for us. My mother says that blue is ____________ best color.

We live under a very nice boy named Joseph. ____________ grandfather made him a blanket.

I hope we stay here for a long time.

Your best friend,
Marty Mouse

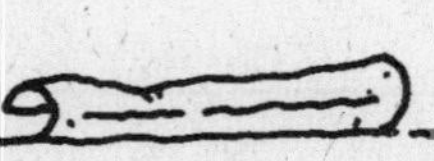

Name ______________________________

Family Tales

Plan your paragraph. Draw or write your ideas.

Who will you write about?

What will you tell about? Draw or write three ideas.

Name

Blanket Match

Each Spelling Word has the vowel sound in ☾ or the vowel sound in 📖.

Spelling Words		
look	took	soon
too	good	food

Your Own Words

Write each Spelling Word on the blanket that has the matching vowel sound.

☾

1 ____________

2 ____________

3 ____________

📖

4 ____________

5 ____________

6 ____________

Write the two Spelling Words that end like 🛏.

7 ____________

8 ____________

Name ______________________

Spelling Spree

Spelling Words		
look	took	soon
too	good	food

Write the missing Spelling Words to finish each news story title. Begin each word with a capital letter.

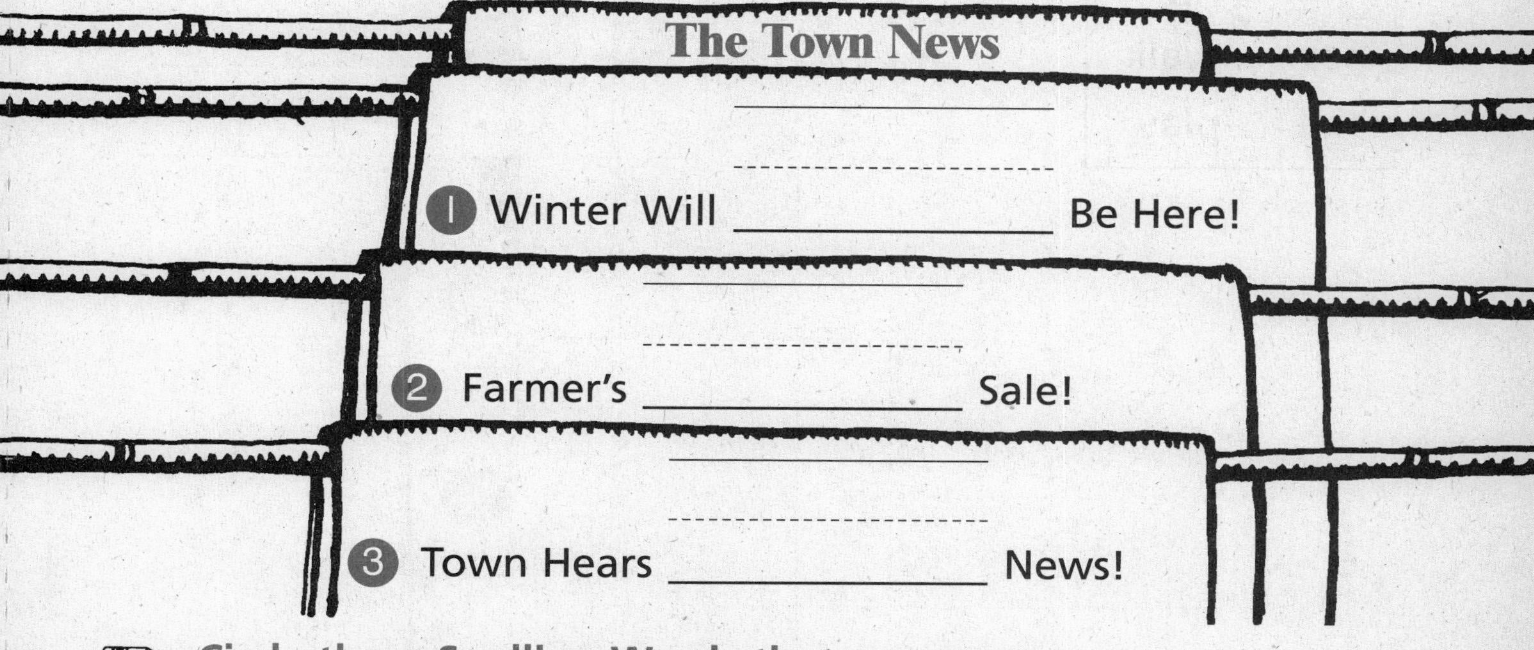

1. Winter Will ______________ Be Here!
2. Farmer's ______________ Sale!
3. Town Hears ______________ News!

Circle three Spelling Words that are wrong. Write each word correctly.

4 ______________  ______________  ______________

Name

Into Action!

Write a word from the box for each picture clue. Add **ed** to tell about the past.

wash	look
sew	walk
roll	play

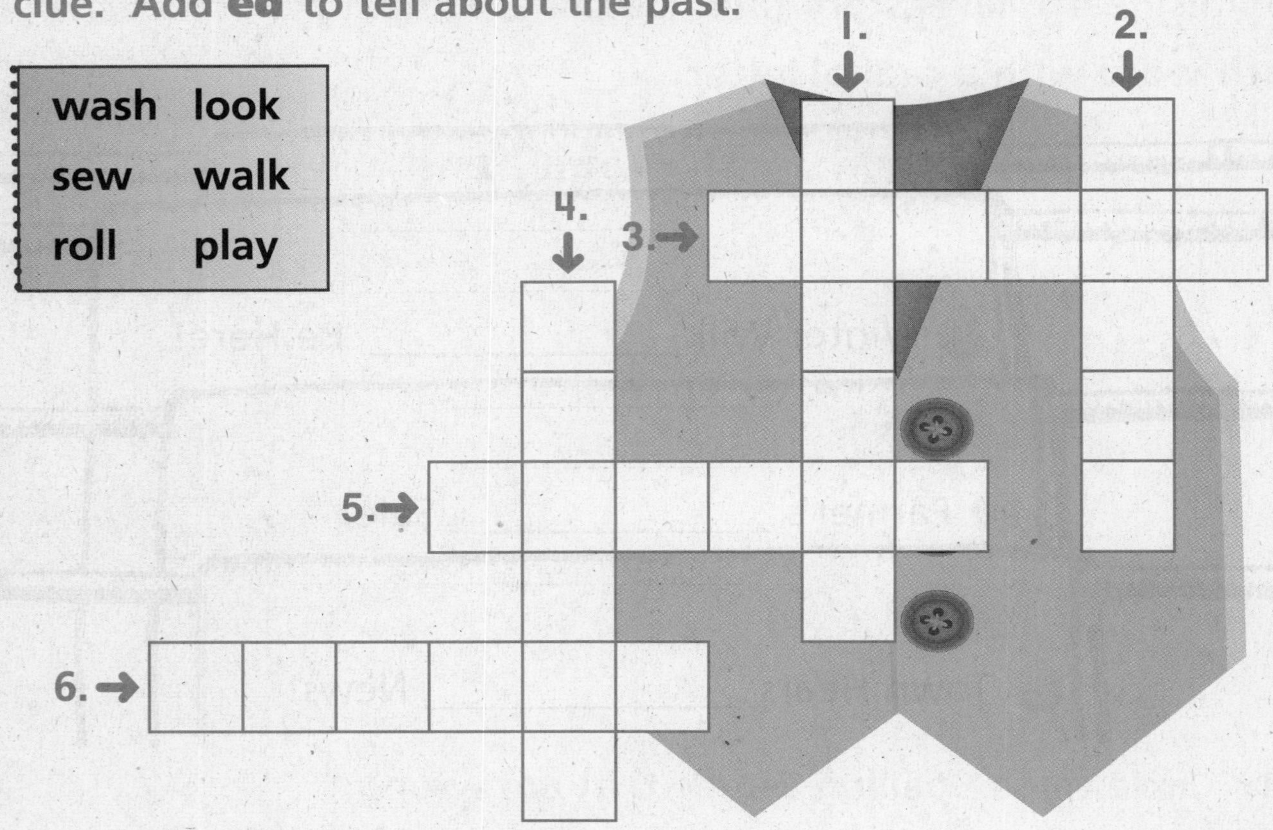

1 

2 

3 

4 

5 

6 

Name

Family Crossword

Complete the puzzle with words from the list. The clues will help you choose the words.

apartment	Mama	Daddy
hand	sister	

Across

2. a kind of home

4. a name for Father

Down

1. You want to help, so you give a ____.

3. a name for Mother

5. not your brother, but your ____

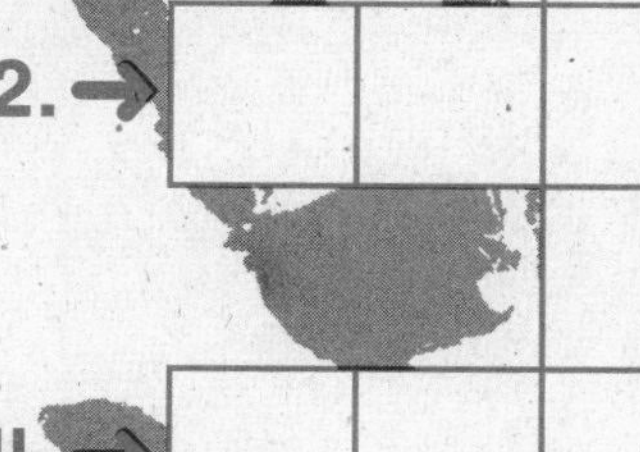

1. 2. 3. 4. 5.

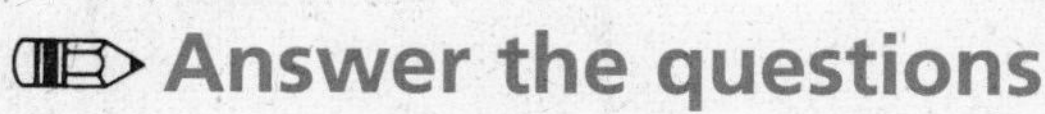

Answer the questions.

Do you have a sister or a brother? ____

Who keeps you company when you are sad?

____

Name

Together

What does the girl who tells the story do with her sisters and with her mama and daddy? Write to tell about it.

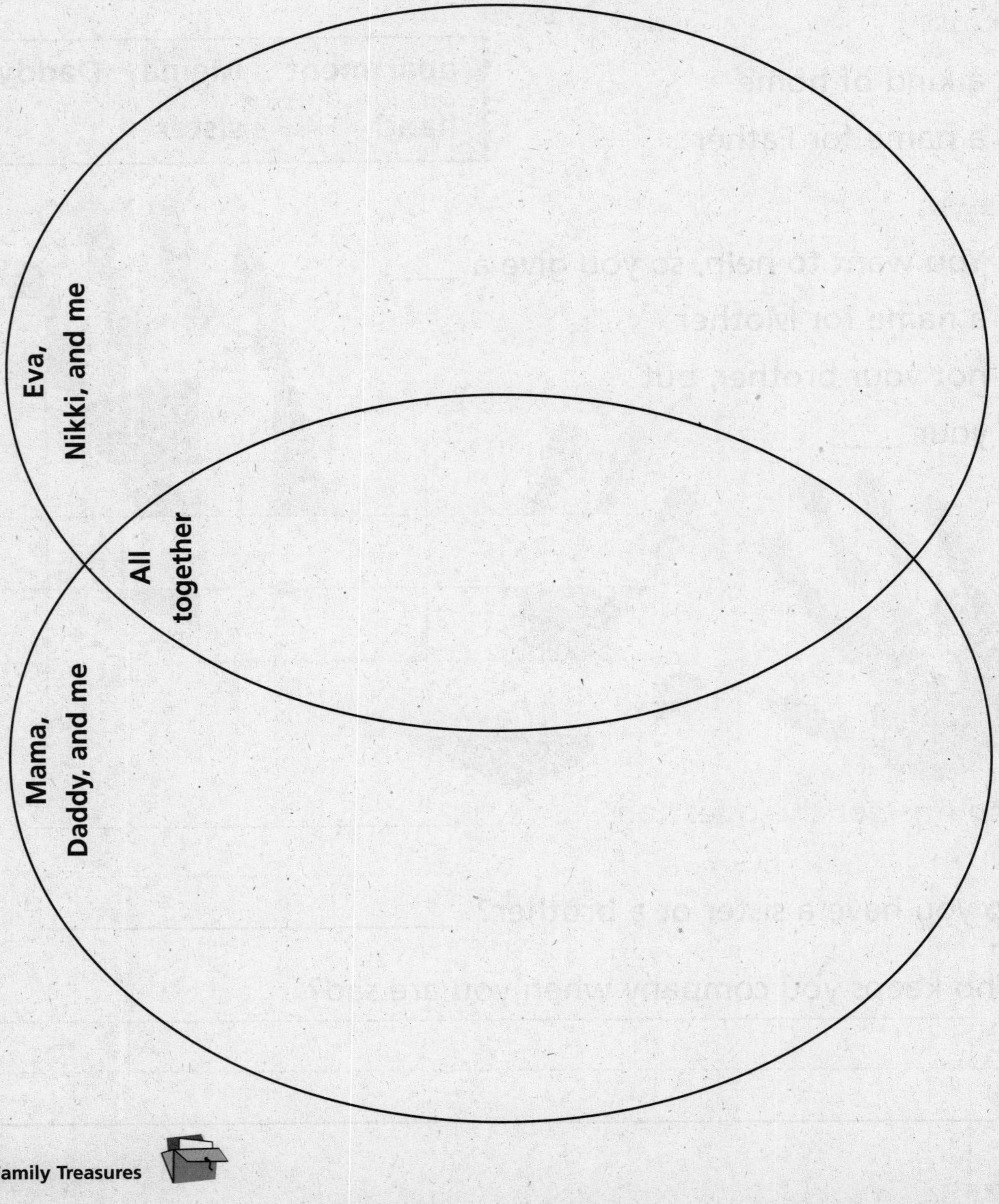

Eva, Nikki, and me

All together

Mama, Daddy, and me

Name ______________________

Three Brothers

Use words from the boxes to complete the sentences about the picture.

1 The three brothers are going ______________________.

home   to school   to work

2 They will get there ______________________.

by walking   in a car   in a bus

3 The children will ______________________ when they get there.

read books   go fishing   see Dad

Write a new sentence about the picture.

4 ______________________

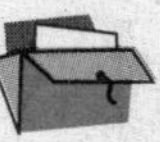

Name ________________________________

A Story for Little Sister

Add an ending to finish each word in the story.
Write each letter on its own line.

ed	ly	s	ing	er	ful	est	y

1 is start ____ ____ ____ slow ____ ____.

2 run ____ fast ____ ____.

3 want ____ ____ to be help ____ ____ ____.

4 is 's great ____ ____ ____ fan.

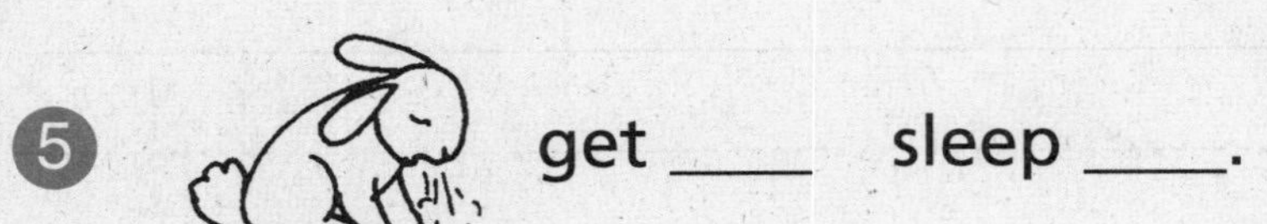

5 get ____ sleep ____.

6 win ____!!!

Name

Three by Three

Cut out the three parts of each sentence. Then put them in order so they make sense. Paste each sentence in its box.

I have	of sister.	the best kind
to hold	I want	her hand.
as a sister	and a friend!	I will keep her

Name

One of Two Sisters

Read each sentence. Draw a line under the contraction. Write the two words that make up the contraction.

1. I'm one of two sisters.

2. Sometimes it's fun to be one of two.

3. But sometimes it isn't so much fun.

4. My little sister can't play many games.

5. But she'll grow up some day.

Name ______________________

All About Me

Read the sentences. Write **I** or **me** to finish each sentence.

1. _______ have two sisters.
2. My sisters and _______ ride the subway.
3. My sisters hold hands with _______.
4. They tell _______ when it is time to get off.

Write about your family. Use the words **I** and **me** in your sentences.

____

____

____

____

Name

More Than One

Spelling Words		
names	seats	steps
days	cans	kites

Your Own Words

Each Spelling Word is a naming word. What letter makes these words mean more than one?

Look at the people and things on this street. Color the pictures that go with each Spelling Word.

Write the Spelling Words that name the pictures you colored. Then draw a line under the letter that makes each word mean more than one.

1 ______________ 3 ______________ 5 ______________

2 ______________ 4 ______________ 6 ______________

Name

Spelling Spree

Spelling Words		
names	seats	steps
days	cans	kites

Write the Spelling Word for each clue.

1 Bikes have them.

2 You put trash in them.

3 You walk up and down them.

Circle three Spelling Words that are wrong. Write each word correctly.

Dear Mr. Lowen,
Thank you for the daisies. They lasted for dayes. We put them on the front steps next to our kytes. We hope you get our naims right next time.
All Three Sisters

4

5

6

Name ______________________________

Pick the Daisies

What word can take the place of each naming word? Write **he**, **she**, or **it** on the right daisy.

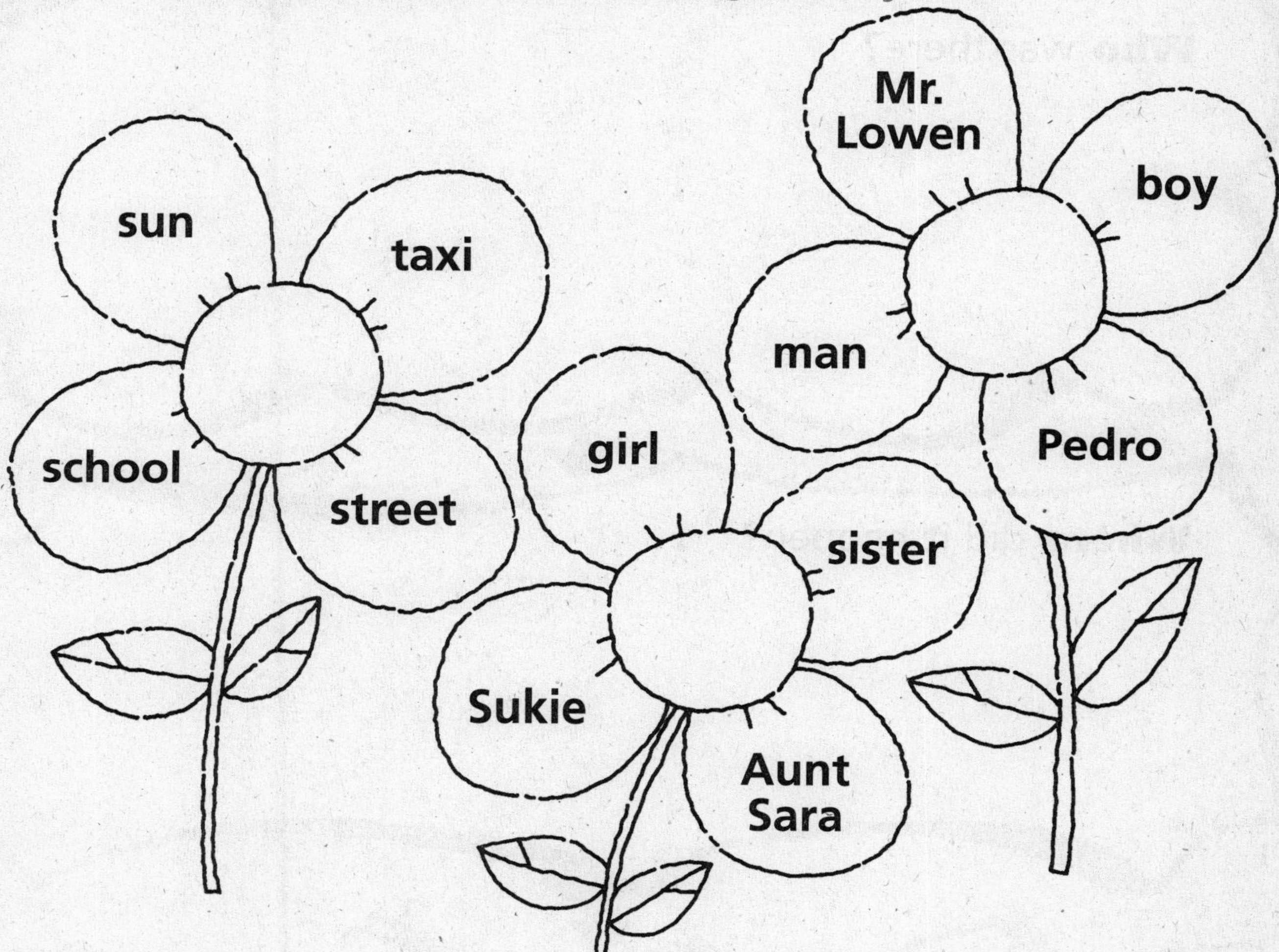

Write this sentence another way. Use a word that can take the place of the underlined words.

<u>The girls</u> get daisies.

____

Name

Who? Where? What?

Write or draw your ideas for your story.

Who was there?

Where did it happen?

What happened?

Name ______________________

Take Another Look

Revising Checklist

Answer these questions about your story.

- ☐ Does my story make sense?
- ☐ Did I tell things in order?

What can I add to my story to make it better?

____

____

____

Questions to Ask My Writing Partner

- What do you like best about my story?
- Did I tell enough?
- Is there anything I should add?

Name ____________________

Making a Flap Story

Look back at **One of Three**. Reread the part where the little sister is sad. Think about a time when you were sad.

Why did you feel sad? ____________________

____

Who in your family helped you feel better? ____________________

____

What did they do? ____________________

____

Make a flap story.

1. Fold a sheet of paper in half.
2. Draw three lines across the front.
3. Cut on the lines to make four flaps.
4. Write **First**, **Next**, **Then**, and **Last** on the flaps.
5. Draw a picture and write a sentence under each flap.

First Next Then

Check your work.

- ☐ My story shows how someone helped me when I was sad.
- ☐ I wrote **First**, **Next**, **Then**, and **Last**.
- ☐ I drew my pictures in order.

Name

Something's Fishy

Think about **Fishy Facts**. Write the topic. Read the main idea. Add details that tell more about the main idea.

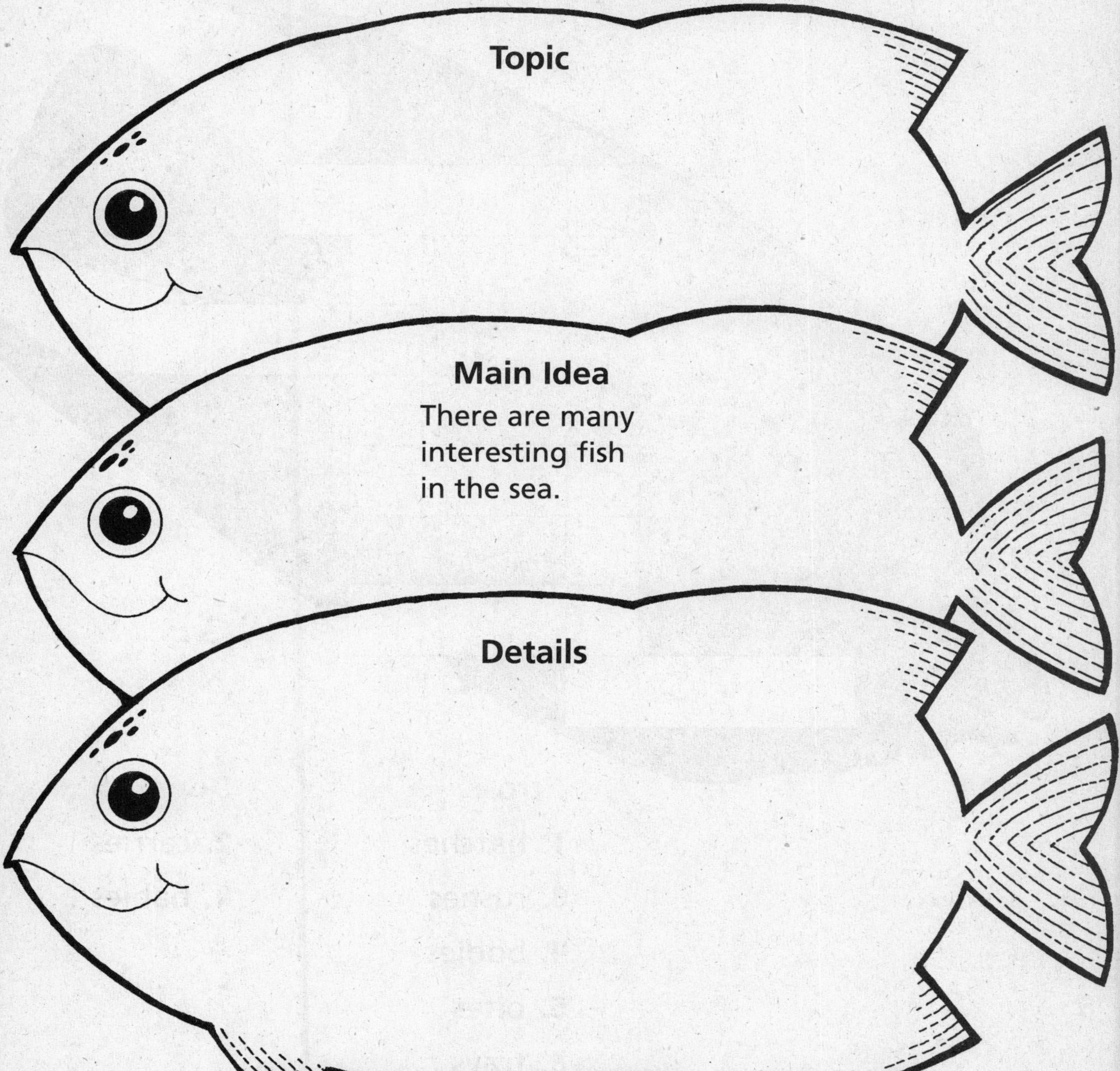

Topic

Main Idea

There are many interesting fish in the sea.

Details

Name

Fishy Crossword

Read each word. Write its base word in the boxes with the same number.

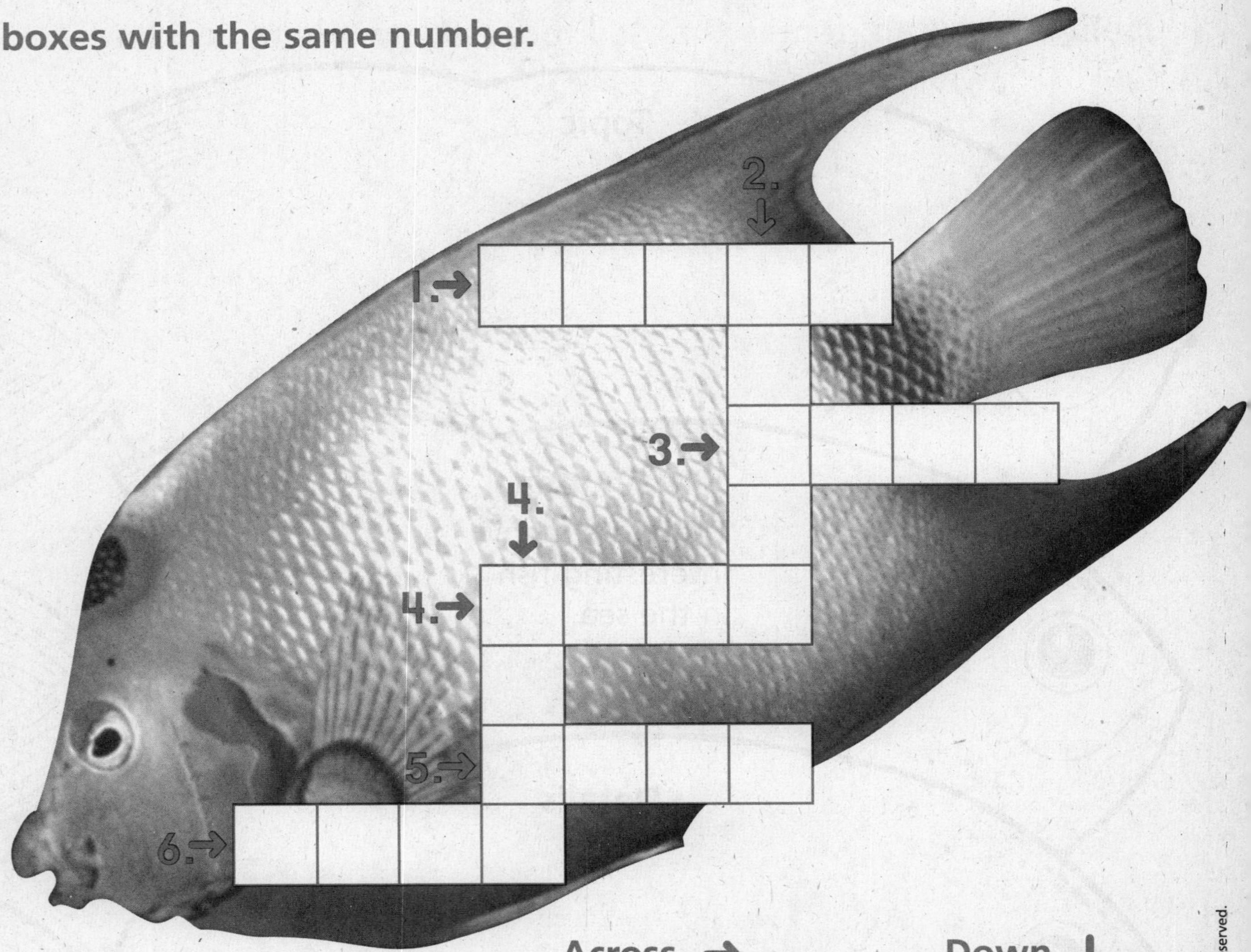

1.→ 2.↓ 3.→ 4.↓ 4.→ 5.→ 6.→

Across 

1. hatches

3. rushes

4. bodies

5. bites

6. trays

Down ↓

2. carries

4. babies

Did you do all this for me?

Guppies, you are great!

HAPPY BIRTHDAY, MRS. SEAHORSE!

SURPRISE!

(Fold Line)

This Is My Book

The Busy Guppies

The Guppies next door are working very hard.

Dad Guppy bakes tarts. Mom Guppy mixes berries and peaches together.

(Fold Line)

Will someone tell me why the Guppies are doing so many things?

(Fold Line)

Big Guppy plants seeds. He tries to plant them all.

The Guppy brothers throw things out in boxes. They are clean little guppies!

(Fold Line)

The Guppy sisters try on new dresses. They never looked happier.

Name ______________________

Fishy Clues

Look at the pictures.
Write a word to finish each sentence.

Which	air	same
only	tell	

1	This fish takes in water or __________ until it gets very big.
2	It's hard to __________ the head from the tail on this fish.
3	These fish look the __________. They seem to like each other!
4	This fish stings __________ when it is afraid.
5	__________ fish is this?

Which fish do you like best? Draw and tell about it.

Name ______________________________

Fishing by ABC's

Cut out each piece. Paste the fish words in ABC order by the diver's head. Paste the shell words in ABC order in the net.

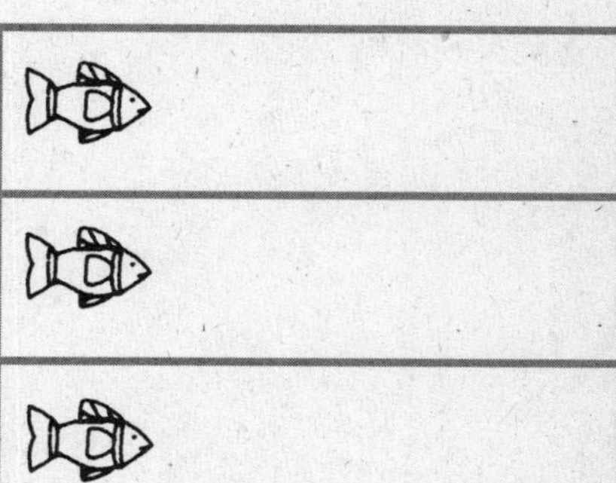

Now go back and read the hidden messages!

water	play	under
fish	home	bring

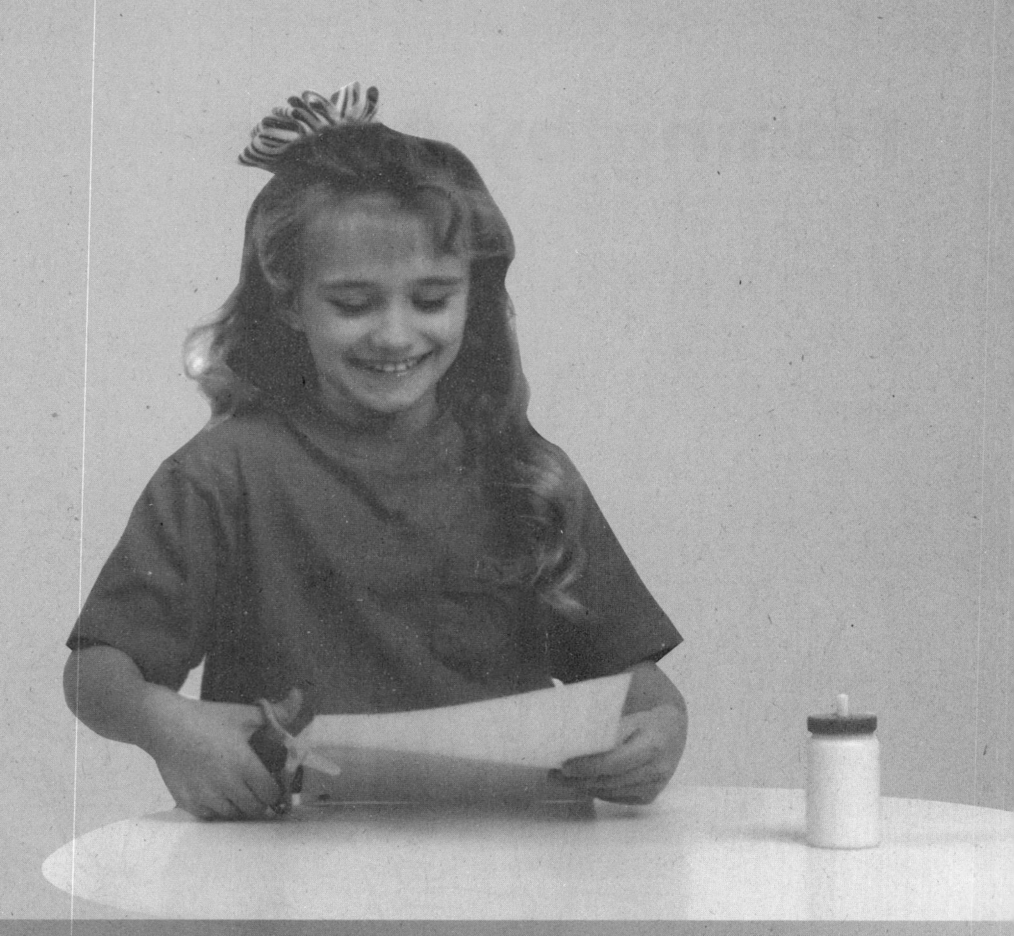

Name ______________________________

What Are They Doing?

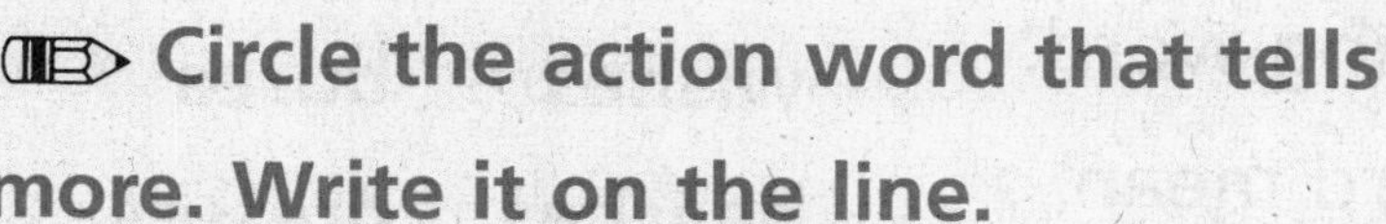

Circle the action word that tells more. Write it on the line.

moved swam

1 The fish ______ away. ______________________

went ran

2 Kelly ______ to look at it. ______________________

said shouted

3 "It's swimming away!" she ______. ______________________

Write two more sentences about the picture. Use clear action words.

____

____

____

Name

Go Fish!

Each Spelling Word is a naming word. Which letters make each word mean more than one?

Spelling Words	
kisses	boxes
wishes	buses
beaches	dresses

Your Own Words

Add **es** to make each Spelling Word mean more than one.

1 ______________________ 4 ______________________

2 ______________________ 5 ______________________

3 ______________________ 6 ______________________

Write the Spelling Word that begins like each picture name.

7  ______________________

8  ______________________

Name

Spelling Spree

Spelling Words	
kisses	boxes
wishes	buses
beaches	dresses

Write the Spelling Word that belongs in each group.

1 cars, trucks, ____

2 cakes, candles, ____

3 shirts, pants, ____

Circle three Spelling Words that are wrong. Write each word correctly.

4 Grunts give kises. ____

5 Buy two boxis of fish food. ____

6 These shells are from beeches around the world. ____

Name

Fishing Line

Color the fish that are alike in the same color.

Each kind of fish should be a different color.

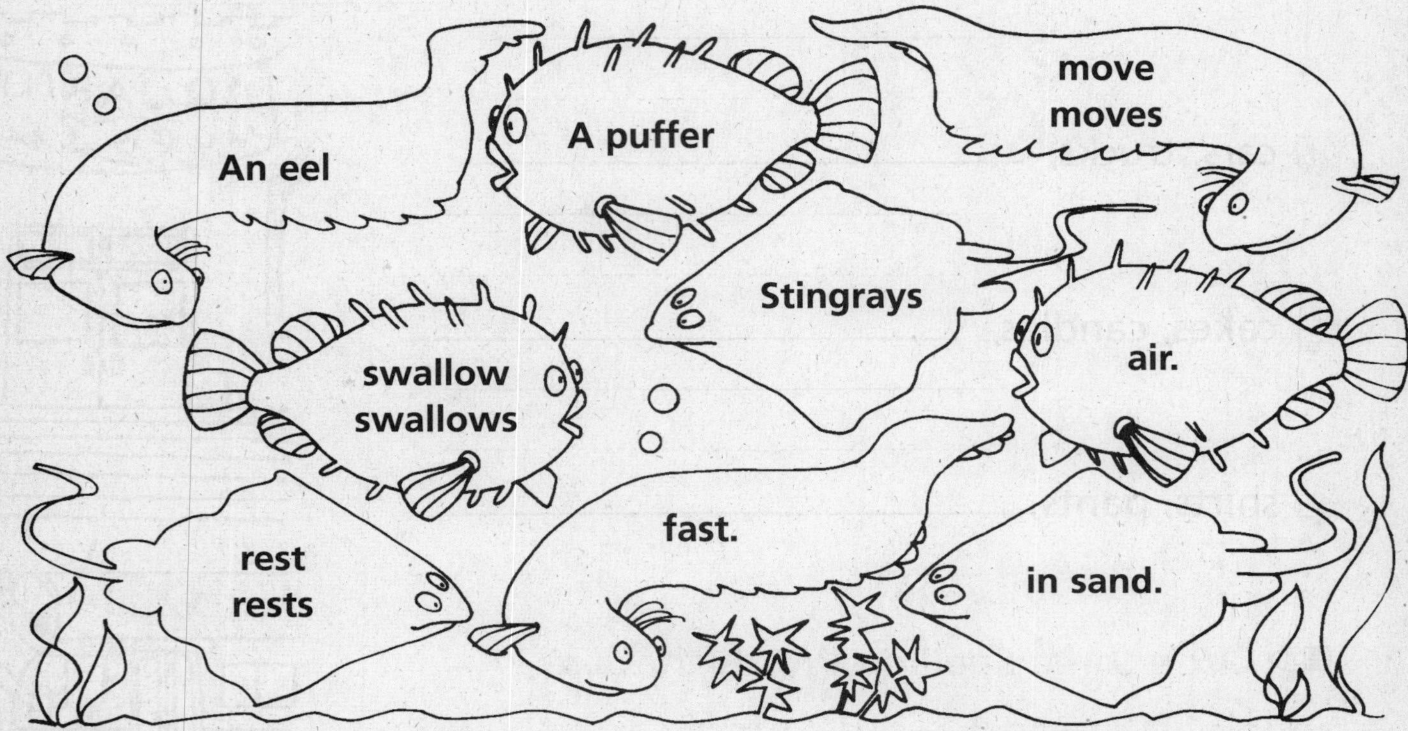

Use words on fish of the same color to write sentences.

Choose the right action word.

1 ____________________

2 ____________________

3 ____________________

Name ______________________

What Is It?

surprise	know
around	wait
must	

Complete each sentence.

1 A boy took a walk ______________________ his house.

2 He found a ______________________.

3 He said, "I don't ______________________ what it is."

4 "I can't ______________________ to find out."

5 "I ______________________ look inside." He looked. It was a fish!

The boy wants the fish to perform tricks. On another sheet of paper, draw pictures to show what feats you would like the fish to do.

Name

A Goldfish Gift

Think about **Enzo the Wonderfish**.

Draw the missing pictures.

1 Mother and Father gave me a fish.

2 I took the fish for a walk.

3 "Can you try this?" I asked.

4 The fish jumped out.

Tell how the story ended.

Name

What's Next?

Read the sentences. Draw what happens next.

A dog sits under a tree.
A cat walks by.
They look at each other.

What's next?

A cat sits by the water.
A fish is in the water.
The cat sees the fish.

What's next?

Now read this.

A boy is in school. His dog waits outside. The boy comes out.

Write what happens next.

Name ______________________

Go Fish!

Add the endings to the base words.

Write the new words.

ing
bake
____

ed
shop
____

est
fast
____

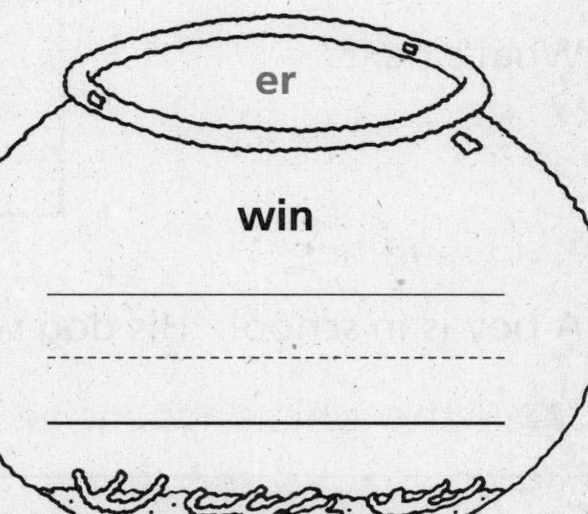

er
win
____

Write a sentence using a word you made.

____

One dog is spinning.

And that dog is WINNING!

(Fold Line)

This Is My Book

The Dog Show

THE DOG SHOW

The dog show is about to start.

Don't the dogs look great?

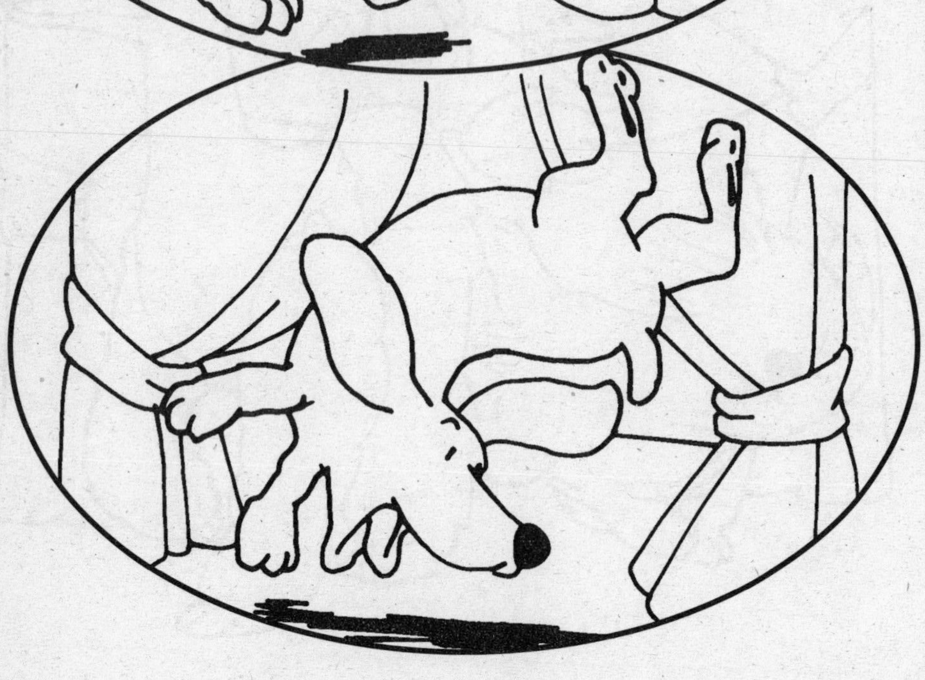

One dog is skipping.

One dog is flipping.

(Fold Line)

One dog is sledding.

One dog is shedding.

One dog is shaving.

(Fold Line)

One dog is baking.

One dog is shaking.

(Fold Line)

One dog is waving.

Name ______________________________

Isn't This Fun?

Read the contractions. Then write the two words that make up each contraction.

Example:

isn't   i s   n o t

1. she'll ___ ___ ___   ___ ___ ___ ___
2. you're ___ ___ ___   ___ ___ ___
3. I'll ___   ___ ___ ___ ___
4. shouldn't ___ ___ ___ ___ ___ ___   ___ ___ ___
5. he'd ___ ___   ___ ___ ___ ___ ___

Now use the circled letters to answer the riddle.

a g___ ___ ___fish

Name

Fishy Friends

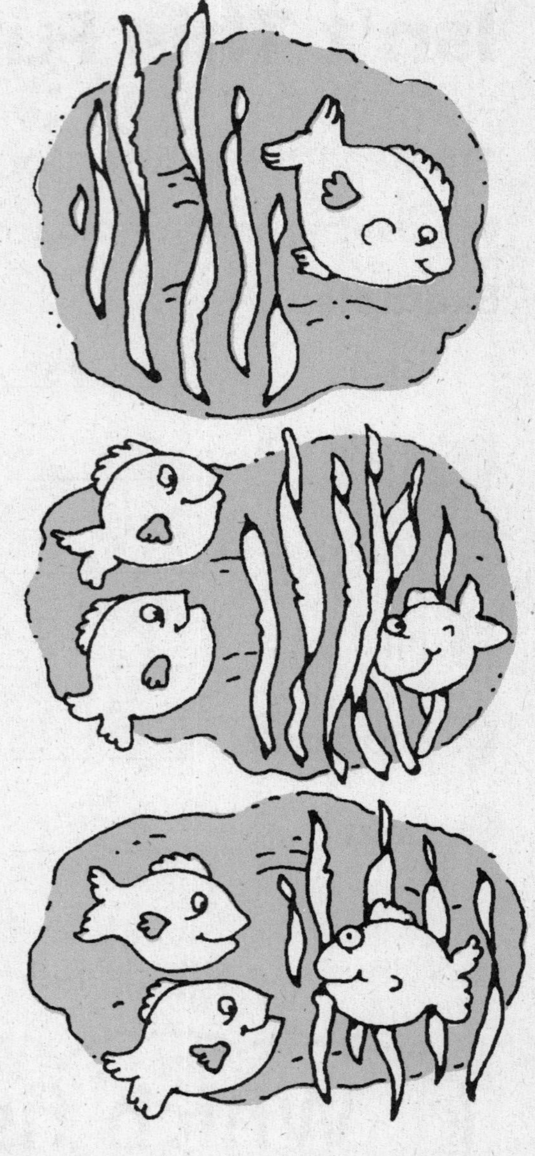

Read the story.

A little fish was in the water. "Who will play with me?" he asked. He had to wait a long time.

Then one more fish came by. "What do you want to play?" she asked.

"I don't know yet," said the little fish. "We must find one more friend."

It took a long time. The two fish looked all around.

Surprise! They found a friend to play with them!

What will the three fish do next?

Name ______________________________

Where Are These Pets?

Cut out and paste the word that names each picture.

Use the other two words to make a new word.
Then turn the page.

walk	doorway	fishpond
side	doghouse	backpack

Write a sentence with the word you made.

Draw a picture to go with it.

Name

Tell Me Why

Think about something you want. Write it in the fishbowl. Write your reasons in the circles.

Name

Jumping Fish

Each Spelling Word is an action word. What ending has been added to each action word?

Draw a line from each word to the ending. Write the Spelling Words you made.

Spelling Words	
looked	jumped
looking	rested
jumping	resting

Your Own Words

look jump rest

ed

1
2
3

look jump rest

ing

4
5
6

Write the two Spelling Words that begin like .

7
8

Name

Spelling Spree

Spelling Words	
looked	jumped
looking	rested
jumping	resting

Write the Spelling Words that go with each clue.

1 sleeping

2 leaped

3 watching

Circle three Spelling Words that are wrong. Write each word correctly.

Fishy News

Yesterday a girl lost her pet fish. She loked for it in her room. The fish had jumped into a cup. The girl put the fish back in its bowl. The fish restid. Today it may do some more jumpin.

4

5

6

Name

What's What?

Draw a line to match the clues with the pictures. Circle the contractions.

1 I can't live in a nest.

I don't have four legs.

2 My home isn't a bowl.

I don't have feathers.

3 I can't use fins to swim.

I don't like to eat hay.

Write two sentences using some of the contractions that you circled.

Name

K-W-L Chart

Write what you know. Write what you want to know. Then write what you have learned.

What I **K**now	What I **W**ant to Know	What I Have **L**earned

Name ____________________

Take Another Look

Revising Checklist

Answer these questions about your report.

- ☐ Did I check my facts?
- ☐ Are there any facts I would like to add?

____

____

Questions to Ask My Writing Partner

- What do you like best about my report?
- Is there anything you didn't understand?
- Have I told enough facts?
- What else would you like to know?

Name ____________________

Look at the Fish!

Cut and paste a word in each box.

Finish the pictures that go with the sentences.

This pretty fish is going [ ] It thinks the plants will make a good home.

There are many [ ] under water. I am happy to see so many great things!

Look at all the water creatures! Here is a [ ] of fish all together.

Some fish have their own homes. This one needs a [ ] to live.

school | away | place | marvels

PASTE

Name ______________________

And Then What?

These sentences about **Swimmy** are mixed up.
Write numbers in the bubbles to tell the right order.

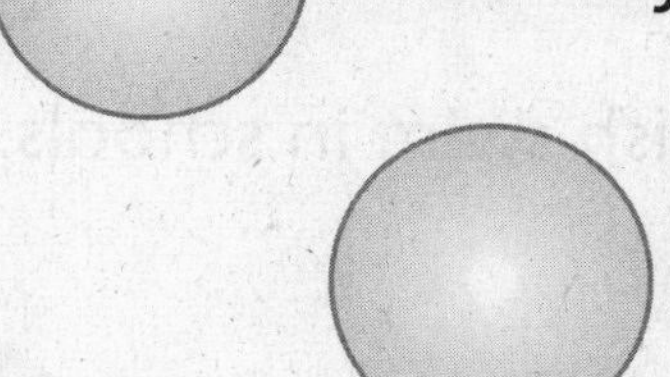

Swimmy found a new school of fish.

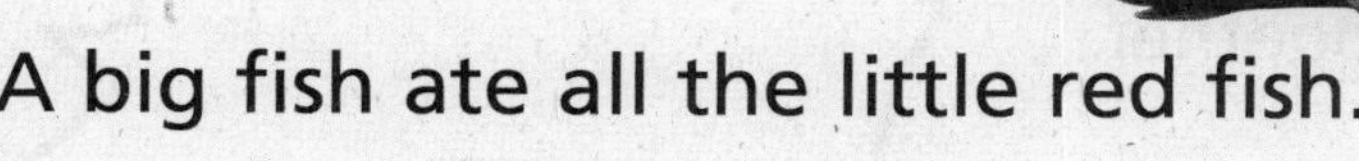

A big fish ate all the little red fish.

Swimmy showed the school how to swim together.

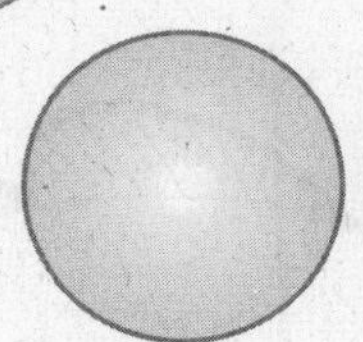

Swimmy was sad and alone.

Write what happened next.

5

Name

Is It Real?

Read each sentence. If it could happen in real life, color the fish red. If it is make-believe, color it yellow.

- Fish walk to school together.
- Fish swim in schools.
- Fish read under the water.
- Some fish live in lakes.
- There are many kinds of water plants.
- People have fish as pets.
- Fish have their own rooms.
- Fish in the sea make things to eat.

Name

Come to a Party!

✂ Cut out the pictures whose names have the **or** or **ar** sound. Paste them on the present.

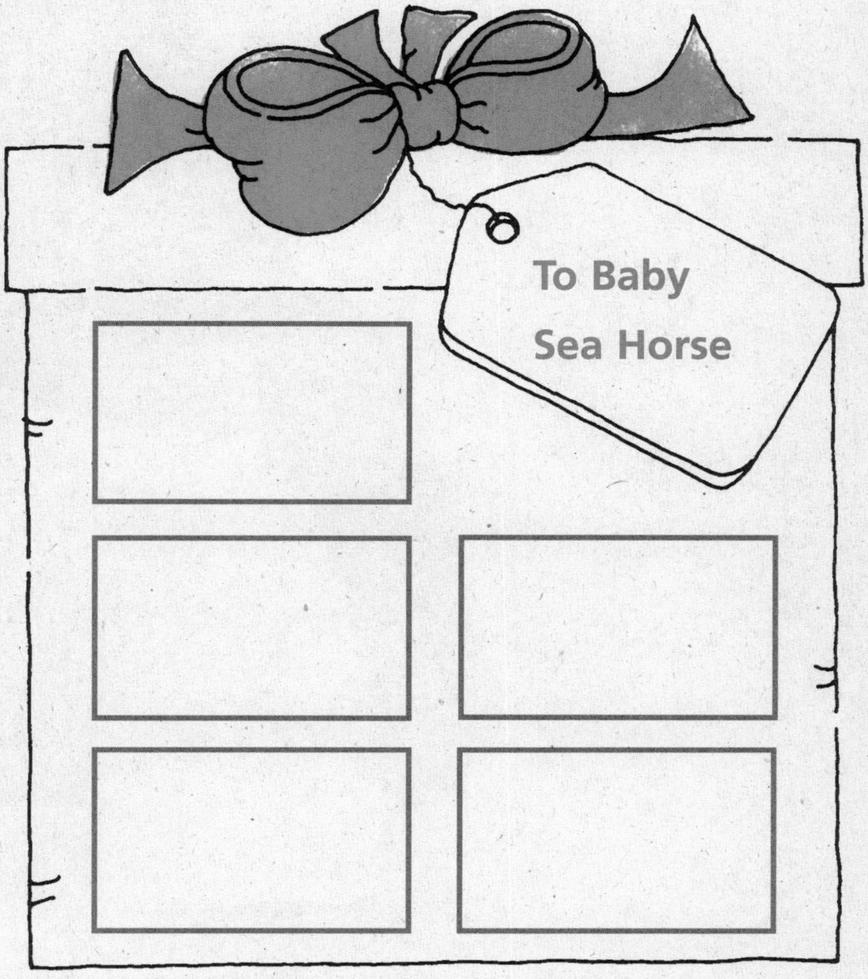

To Baby
Sea Horse

"... a new car!"

(Fold Line)

This Is My Book

Bart and Mort's Hard Day

Bart and Mort wanted some corn. So they went to the store. They saw a pig!

Mort blew the car's horn.

Then the horn wouldn't stop!

(Fold Line)

"Bart!" said Mort. "You go get the corn. I'm going to get . . . "

"The store is not far," said Bart.
"We could walk there."

(Fold Line)

Mort started to park the car, but it
wouldn't turn. The car was in some tar!

Mort turned off the car.

Then sparks came out!

(Fold Line)

"We need some help," said

Mort. "This car won't go."

Name ______________________

Make a Fish

Write the word that best completes each sentence. Then cut out and paste the puzzle pieces on another sheet of paper to make a fish.

away	own	think	happy

They have a place of their ____________.

They don't want Swimmy to go ____________.

The little fish are ____________.

They ____________ Swimmy is great.

Name ______________________________

The Little Fish Who Got Away

Finish the sentences.

together	afraid	school	little

The ______________ fish saw a big fish.

He was ______________.

Then he found a ______________ of more little fish.

They all swam away ______________.

Say the words you wrote. Write the number of syllables above each word.

Name ______________________

About This Book!

Write about a book you have read.

Title: ______________________

Author: ______________________

This book is about ______________________

I like this book because ______________________

Name

Letter Rocks

Spelling Words		
far	hard	car
dark	arm	farm

Your Own Words

Each Spelling Word has a vowel sound that is not short or long. It is the vowel sound you hear at the end of **car**.

Write the missing letters to spell the vowel sound you hear in car. Then write the Spelling Words.

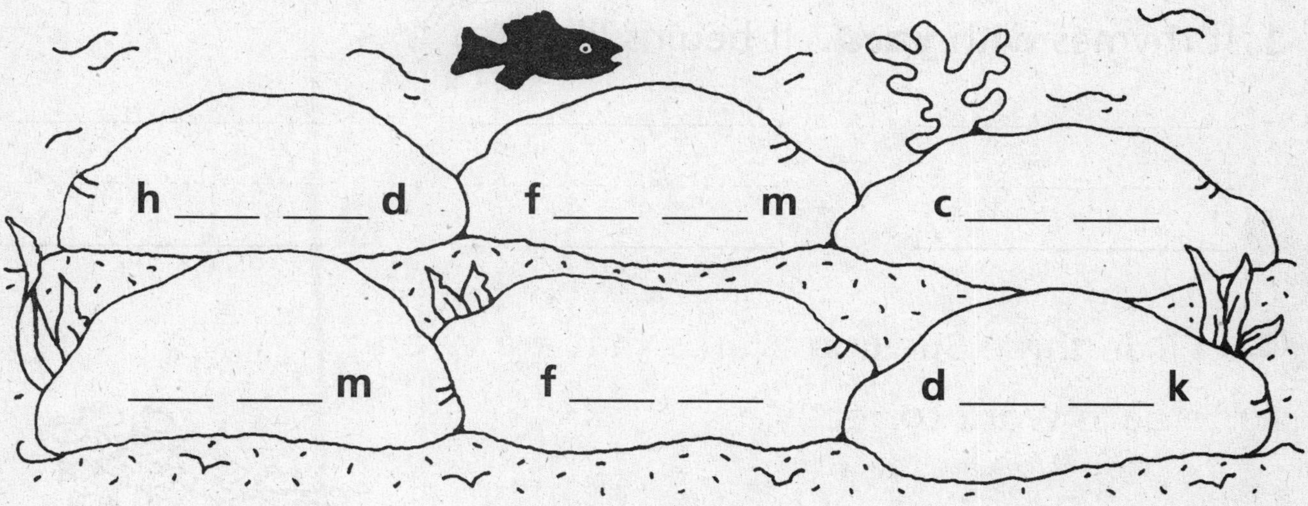

h ___ ___ d   f ___ ___ m   c ___ ___

___ ___ m   f ___ ___   d ___ ___ k

1 ______   3 ______   5 ______

2 ______   4 ______   6 ______

Write the two Spelling Words that rhyme with star.

7 ______   8 ______

Name

Spelling Spree

Spelling Words		
far	hard	car
dark	arm	farm

Write the Spelling Word for each clue.

1. It rhymes with **alarm**. It begins like [fish].
2. It rhymes with **star**. It begins like [cat].
3. It rhymes with **yard**. It begins like [horse].

1 ______ 2 ______ 3 ______

Circle three Spelling Words that are wrong. Write each word correctly.

To: My School Pals
From: Swimmy

- Do not swim farr.
- Do not go into darke caves. It will be hard to see.
- An octopus can grab you with one ahm. Stay away!

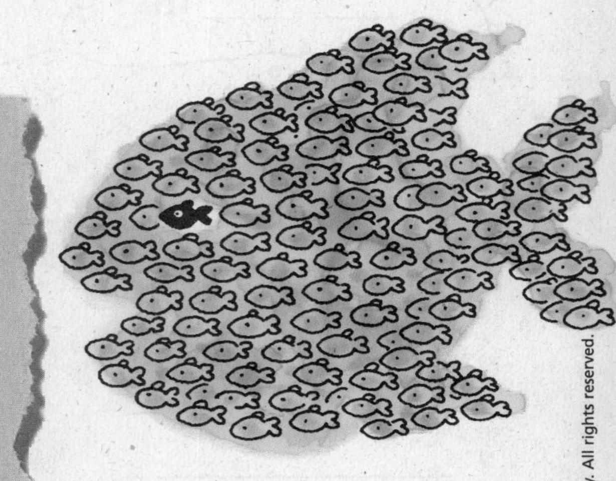

4 ______ 5 ______ 6 ______

Name

Look into Our Eyes

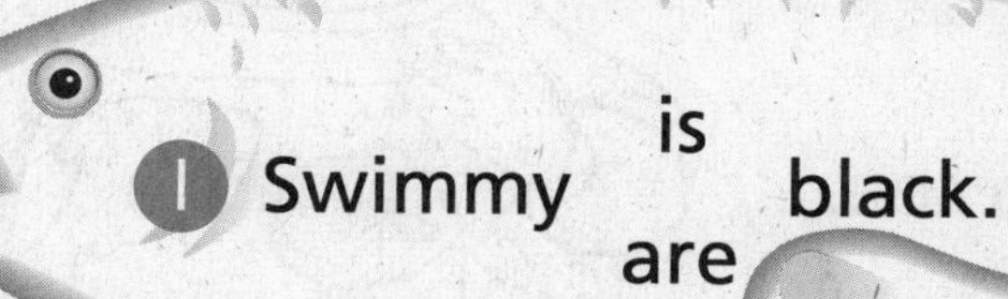

Read the sentences. Draw a circle around the word that makes sense.

1. Swimmy is / are black.
2. The rocks is / are pretty.
3. Those eels was / were long.
4. The sea was / were cold.
5. Some lobsters is / are dark green.

Write a sentence using one of the words you circled.

Name ______________________

Making a Fish Bowl Collage

Read the story and look at the picture.

Kay put her new fish in their home.
"This place is no fun," said Shiny.
"We can't play or hide," said Tiny.
The fish made sad faces for Kay to see.
So Kay went back to the pet shop.

How are Shiny and Tiny like real fish?

____

How are Shiny and Tiny not like real fish?

____

Make cutouts to show what Kay got at the pet shop.

Now make a Fish Bowl Collage to show how Shiny and Tiny's bowl will look.

Check your work.

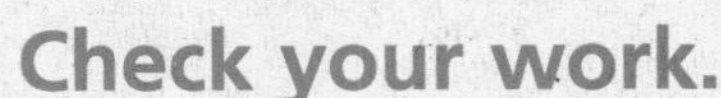

- ☐ My collage shows what Kay got at the pet shop.
- ☐ My collage shows how Shiny and Tiny's home will look.
- ☐ I can tell about **real** and **not real** parts of the story.

MY HANDBOOK

Contents

MY FAVORITE STORIES

Name of Book

Name of Book

Name of Book

Name of Book

Name of Book

Name of Book

Name of Book

MY FAVORITE STORIES

Name of Book

Name of Book

Name of Book

Name of Book

Name of Book

Name of Book

Name of Book

MY FAVORITE STORIES

Name of Book

Name of Book

Name of Book

Name of Book

Name of Book

Name of Book

Name of Book

MY FAVORITE STORIES

Name of Book

Name of Book

Name of Book

Name of Book

Name of Book

Name of Book

Name of Book

Name of Book

Name of Book

Name of Book

Name of Book

Name of Book

Name of Book

Name of Book

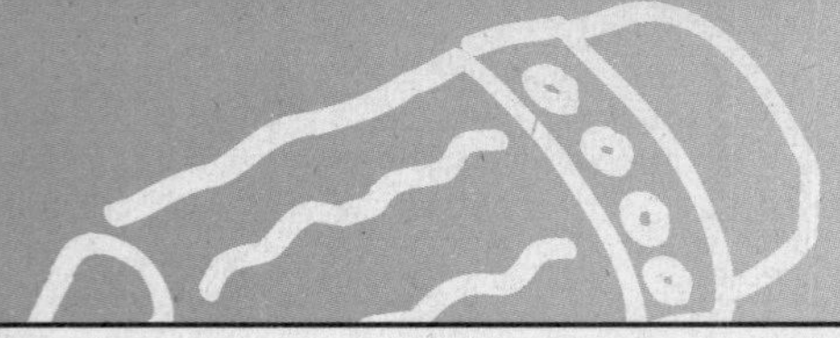

Trace and write the letters.

Aa Aa

Bb Bb

Cc Cc

Dd Dd

Ee Ee

Ff Ff

Gg Gg

McDougal, Littell 1993 Handwriting (continuous stroke)

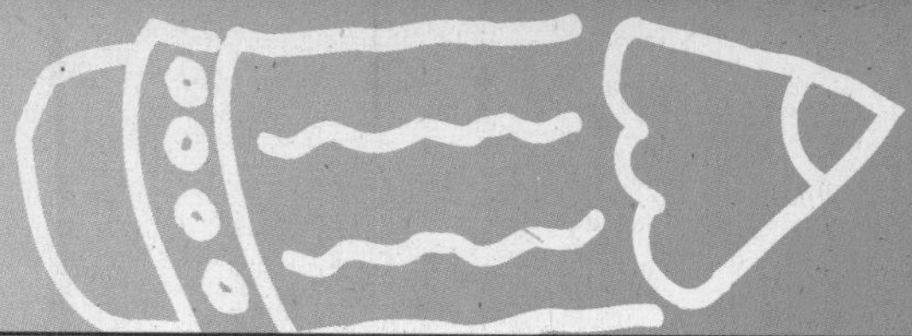

Trace and write the letters.

Hh Hh

Ii Ii

Jj Jj

Kk Kk

Ll Ll

Mm Mm

WRITING THE ALPHABET

Trace and write the letters.

Nn Nn

Oo Oo

Pp Pp

Qq Qq

Rr Rr

Ss Ss

Tt Tt

McDougal, Littell 1993 Handwriting (continuous stroke)

Trace and write the letters.

Uu Uu

Vv Vv

Ww Ww

Xx Xx

Yy Yy

Zz Zz

WRITING THE ALPHABET

Trace and write the letters.

Aa Aa

Bb Bb

Cc Cc

Dd Dd

Ee Ee

Ff Ff

Gg Gg

McDougal, Littell 1990 Handwriting (ball and stick)

Trace and write the letters.

Hh Hh

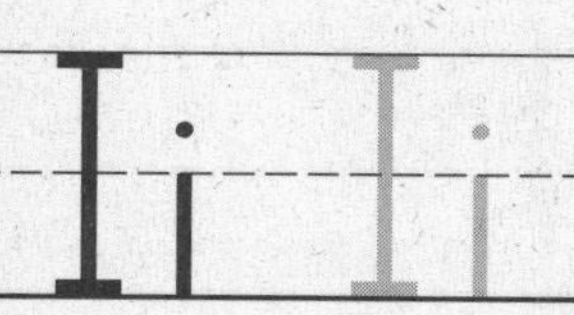
Ii Ii

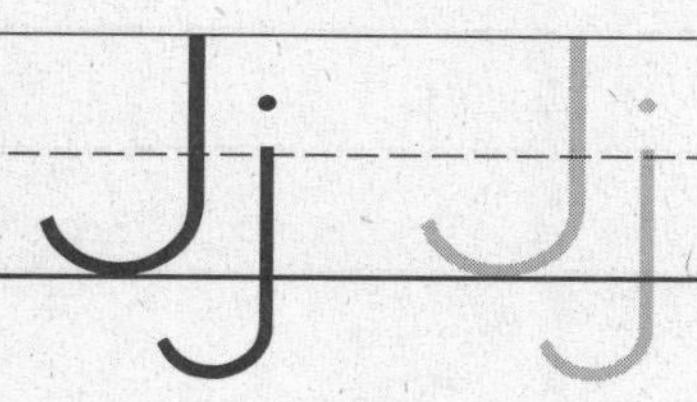
Jj Jj

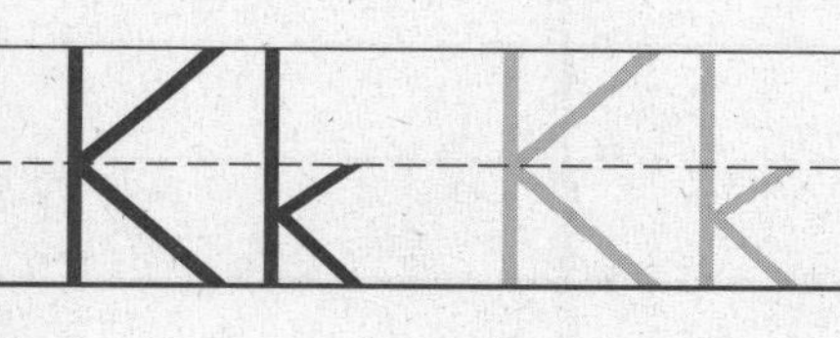
Kk Kk

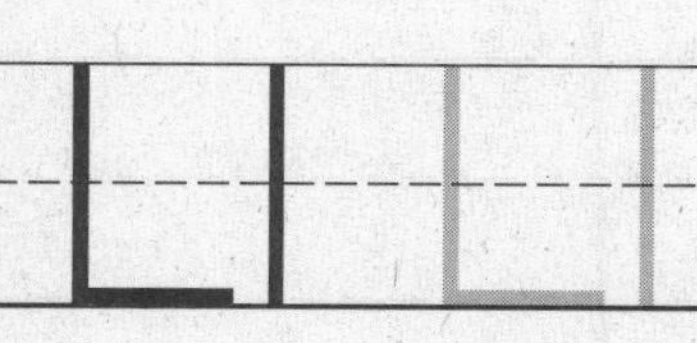
Ll Ll

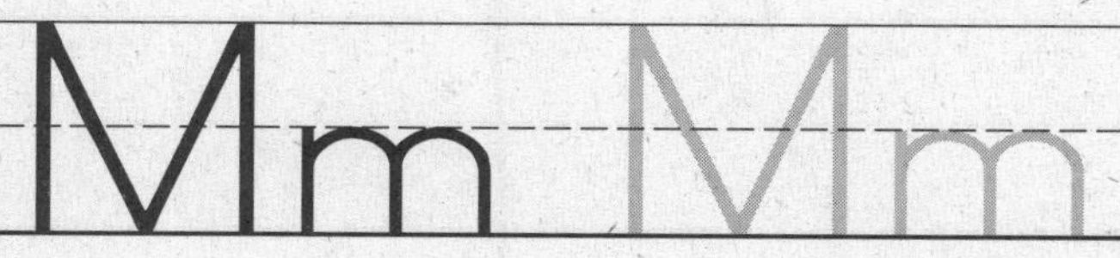
Mm Mm

WRITING THE ALPHABET

Trace and write the letters.

Nn Nn

Oo Oo

Pp Pp

Qq Qq

Rr Rr

Ss Ss

Tt Tt

McDougal, Littell 1990 Handwriting (ball and stick)

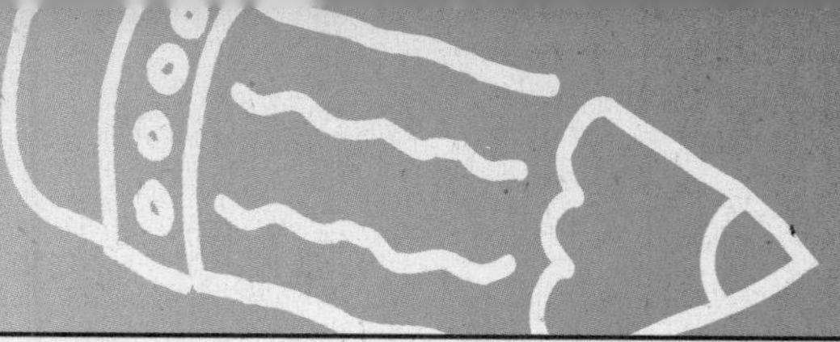

Trace and write the letters.

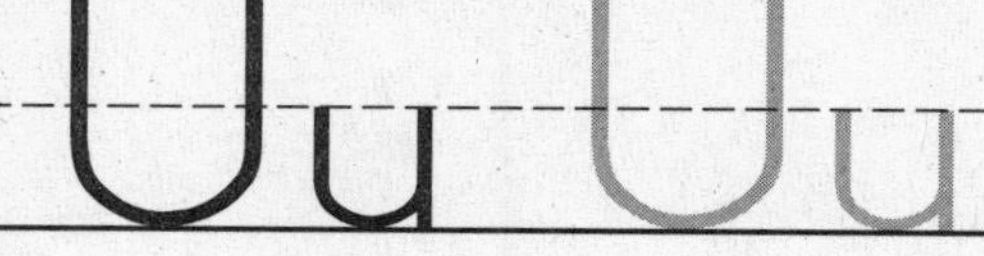

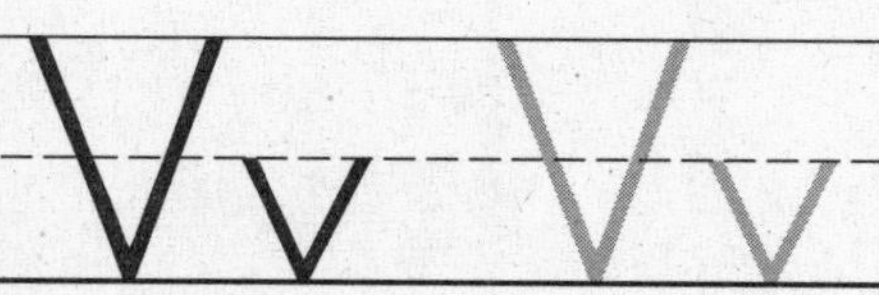

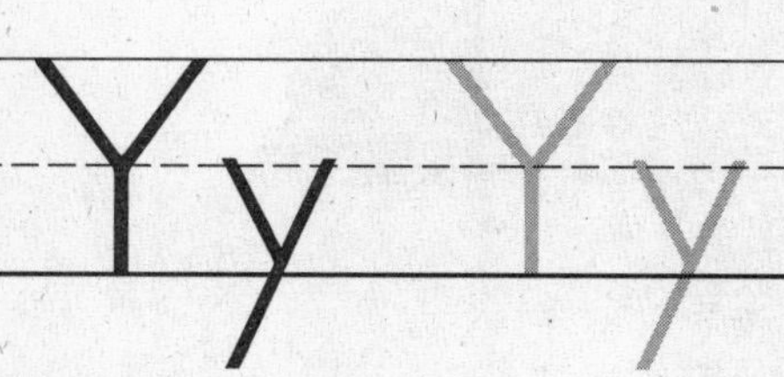

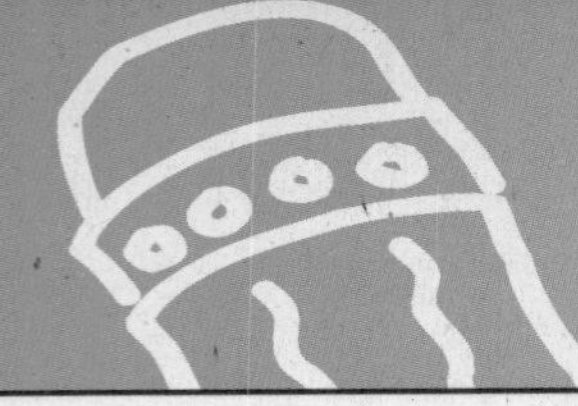

How to Study a Word

1. **LOOK at the word.**
2. **SAY the word.**
3. **THINK about the word.**
4. **WRITE the word.**
5. **CHECK the spelling.**

There's an Alligator Under My Bed

The Long i Sound
time
like
hide

Spelling Words

1. time
2. like
3. hide
4. mine
5. five
6. bike

Challenge Words

1. smile
2. write

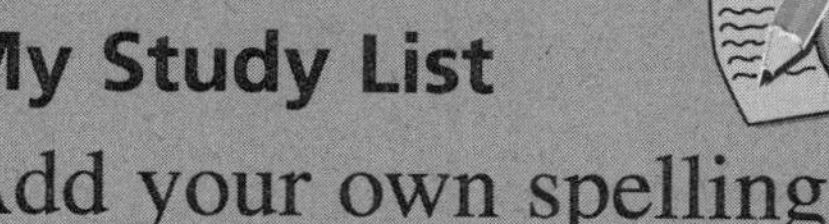

My Study List
Add your own spelling words on the back. →

Take-Home Word Lists

EEK! There's a Mouse in the House

The Long a Sound
cake
late
name

Spelling Words

1. cake
2. make
3. came
4. take
5. late
6. name

Challenge Words

1. chase
2. place

My Study List
Add your own spelling words on the back. →

Name

My Study List

1.

2.

3.

4.

5.

6.

More Story Words

You may want to use these words in your own writing.

1. door
2. ran
3. stop

Spelling and Writing Word Lists

Name

My Study List

1.

2.

3.

4.

5.

6.

More Story Words

You may want to use these words in your own writing.

1. just
2. never
3. sleep

If the Dinosaurs Came Back

The Long e Sound

we

need

tree

Spelling Words

1. we
2. need
3. be
4. tree
5. see
6. me

Challenge Words

1. teeth
2. maybe

My Study List
Add your own spelling words on the back. →

Take-Home Word Lists

If You Give a Moose a Muffin

The Long o Sound

so

bone

joke

Spelling Words

1. go
2. so
3. home
4. no
5. bone
6. joke

Challenge Words

1. close
2. those

My Study List
Add your own spelling words on the back. →

Name ______________________

My Study List

____

1. ______________________

2. ______________________

3. ______________________

4. ______________________

5. ______________________

6. ______________________

More Story Words

You may want to use these words in your own writing.

1. ask
2. give
3. mother

Spelling and Writing Word Lists

Name ______________________

My Study List

____

1. ______________________

2. ______________________

3. ______________________

4. ______________________

5. ______________________

6. ______________________

More Story Words

You may want to use these words in your own writing.

1. about
2. always
3. work

The Tug of War

The Long a Sound
Spelled ay
m**ay**
pl**ay**
st**ay**

Spelling Words

1. day
2. may
3. play
4. say
5. way
6. stay

Challenge Words

1. away
2. today

My Study List
Add your own spelling words on the back. →

George Shrinks

The Long e Sound
Spelled ea
eat
cl**ea**n
r**ea**d

Spelling Words

1. eat
2. clean
3. each
4. read
5. seat
6. mean

Challenge Words

1. please
2. scream

My Study List
Add your own spelling words on the back. →

Name ____________________

My Study List

1. ____________________
2. ____________________
3. ____________________
4. ____________________
5. ____________________
6. ____________________

More Story Words

You may want to use these words in your own writing.

1. brother
2. father
3. water

Spelling and Writing Word Lists

Name ____________________

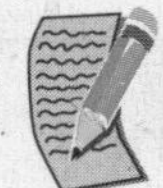

My Study List

1. ____________________
2. ____________________
3. ____________________
4. ____________________
5. ____________________
6. ____________________

More Story Words

You may want to use these words in your own writing.

1. because
2. bring
3. friend

Something from Nothing

The Vowel Sounds in
moon and book
look
good
too
soon

Spelling Words

1. look
2. too
3. took
4. good
5. soon
6. food

Challenge Words

1. shook
2. school

My Study List
Add your own spelling words on the back. →

Take-Home Word Lists

A Mother for Choco

The Long i Sound
Spelled y
my
cry
sky

Spelling Words

1. my
2. cry
3. by
4. try
5. fly
6. sky

Challenge Words

1. why
2. July

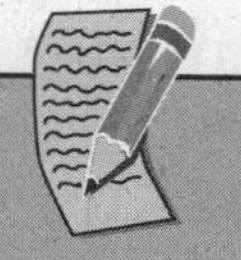

My Study List
Add your own spelling words on the back. →

221

Name

My Study List

1.

2.

3.

4.

5.

6.

More Story Words

You may want to use these words in your own writing.

1. children
2. first
3. gave

Spelling and Writing Word Lists

Name

My Study List

1.

2.

3.

4.

5.

6.

More Story Words

You may want to use these words in your own writing.

1. afraid
2. every
3. school

Fishy Facts

Adding es to Naming Words

kiss**es**

beach**es**

box**es**

Spelling Words

1. kisses
2. wishes
3. beaches
4. boxes
5. buses
6. dresses

Challenge Words

1. pouches
2. bunches

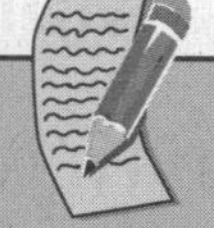

My Study List

Add your own spelling words on the back. →

One of Three

Adding s to Naming Words

name**s**

day**s**

step**s**

Spelling Words

1. names
2. days
3. seats
4. cans
5. steps
6. kites

Challenge Words

1. hands
2. stores

My Study List

Add your own spelling words on the back. →

Name ______________________

My Study List

1. ______________________
2. ______________________
3. ______________________
4. ______________________
5. ______________________
6. ______________________

More Story Words

You may want to use these words in your own writing.

1. keep
2. kind
3. sister

Spelling and Writing Word Lists

Name ______________________

My Study List

1. ______________________
2. ______________________
3. ______________________
4. ______________________
5. ______________________
6. ______________________

More Story Words

You may want to use these words in your own writing.

1. hard
2. same
3. until

Swimmy

The Vowel + r Sound
in car
f**ar**
d**ar**k
f**ar**m

Spelling Words

1. far
2. dark
3. hard
4. arm
5. car
6. farm

Challenge Words

1. are
2. marvel

My Study List
Add your own spelling words on the back. →

Take-Home Word Lists

Enzo the Wonderfish

Adding ed **and** ing
look**ed**
look**ing**
rest**ed**
rest**ing**

Spelling Words

1. looked
2. looking
3. jumped
4. jumping
5. rested
6. resting

Challenge Words

1. floated
2. floating

My Study List
Add your own spelling words on the back. →

Spelling and Writing Word Lists

Name ______________________

My Study List

1. ______________________
2. ______________________
3. ______________________
4. ______________________
5. ______________________
6. ______________________

More Story Words

You may want to use these words in your own writing.

1. around
2. know
3. surprise

Spelling and Writing Word Lists

Name ______________________

My Study List

1. ______________________
2. ______________________
3. ______________________
4. ______________________
5. ______________________
6. ______________________

More Story Words

You may want to use these words in your own writing.

1. away
2. happy
3. place

1. Here are two ways to spell the long **a** sound.

   cake stay

2. The long **e** sound may be spelled **e**, **ee**, or **ea**.

   we need read

3. Here are two ways to spell the long **i** sound.

   time cry

4. Here are two ways to spell the long **o** sound.

   so bone

5. The vowel sounds in **moon** and **book** are spelled **oo**.

   too good

6. The vowel + **r** sound may be spelled **ar**.

   far dark

7. Add **s** or **es** to most naming words to mean more than one.

   days boxes

8. Add **ed** or **ing** to some action words without changing the spelling.

   looked looking

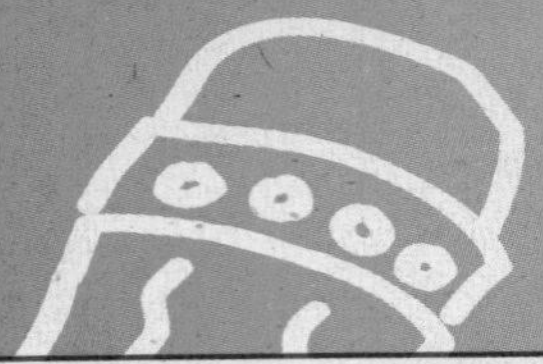

PROOFREADING CHECKLIST

Answer these questions when you check your writing.

- ☐ Did I begin each sentence with a capital letter?
- ☐ Did I use the right mark at the end of each sentence? (. ?)
- ☐ Did I spell each word correctly?

Proofreading Marks		
^	Add	My aunt came ^to visit.
—	Take out	We ~~were~~ sang songs.